Healers and Heroes

Healers and Heroes

WWII Combat Medics: Mud and Blood from the Normandy Beaches to The Battle of the Bulge

Featuring frontline accounts by

Robert T. Marshall
and
Walter German

Edited by

Thea Marshall

1564 PUBLISHING

1564 Publishing, Honolulu HI

Ordering Information:
Quantity sales: Special discounts are available on quantity purchases by corporations, associations, and others.

Heroes and Healers / Thea Marshall. —1st ed.

Library of Congress Control Number: 2019905395

ISBN # 978-0-9600575-1-1

Whose woods they were we couldn't know,
Perhaps a villager's below.
Our task: to search them far and near,
Slewing thru the cold hard snow.

Our litter jeep was hard to steer;
At times the trail would disappear
Among the trees; while up ahead
The mortar rounds burst loud and clear.

Our point was pinned. One man was dead,
Two others bleeding; so we spread
And searched in ever widening sweep
With alternating hope and dread.

The woods were deadly, dark and deep,
But then we found them; with our jeep
We racked them safely to our keep,
We racked them safely to our keep.

R. T. Marshall
Medical Admin. Officer, WWII

[With apologies to Robert Frost]

For Dad and Mom

+ + +

Contents

Introduction

HEALERS AND HEROES is a story of ordinary people behaving in extraordinary ways.

Does each of us have that capacity to be heroic and healing? Based on four years' involvement with this book, and after much WWII research, my answer is a resounding "Yes!"

Healers and Heroes began as a labor of love but quickly developed into a fascination with the content. How were these young WWII soldiers able to be healers and heroes? Was it military training, upbringing, genetics, some other mysterious force? Nature or nurture? A combination of the two? Other factors I'd not yet considered?

Often, these men and women were really just kids, fresh from factories and steel mills and farms, from schools and universities, from towns and cities across America. Yet they answered their country's call and triumphed against an evil so horrific and frightening, many refused to speak of it for decades afterward.

What was the source of their courage and decency? How can such traits be learned and cultivated?

This account of a small medical unit during WWII is necessarily limited in scope, but its very specificity provides a rich, detailed tapestry that allows the reader to identify with the characters. There's no wallowing or chest-thumping, just young soldiers, choosing to persevere and do the right thing despite often being scared, cold and confused.

Pithy, pragmatic, and with a dash of humor, *Healers and Heroes* tells how it happened.

My late mother, Ann Hall Marshall, asked me to publish my Dad's memoirs—I agreed, of course, honored by her trust. I had produced Mom's debut novel when she was 89 years old (2010)— that book, *Crooked Lines*, received a Writer's Digest award and was #1 in its Amazon genre on her 90th birthday. I brought out her second novel the next year.

In 2015, Mom and I continued our collaboration. I figured Dad's project would be fairly straightforward—have the WWII manuscript (re-typed by my father in the mid-1990s) scanned, cleaned up, and edited—then good to go.

Wrong!

I started by re-reading my Dad's memoirs, which began when he was born in Johnstown, PA and covered through age 75 in Emmitsburg, MD.

Although well-written and entertaining, I concluded that Dad's autobiography would be mainly of interest to his family. And it would take serious work to whip it into shape.

Instead, I proposed to my mother that we focus on the WWII section, written in Czechoslovakia after hostilities had ceased. I thought the WWII story could engage a wider audience.

Mom agreed enthusiastically—she loved to go big.

This book led me a merry chase. Frequently, a challenging merry chase.

Preparing a 70-year-old, un-chaptered military manuscript for publication, with both the main author and his co-author long gone, is quite an undertaking.

Potholes slowed the path to publication.

Despite obstacles galore (a few noted in the *Afterword*), I persevered because the stories of WWII must never be forgotten.

The lessons from that legacy of honor and devotion should be held close to our hearts.

With slogging, brave progress, the Allied Forces wrested democracy from the jaws of tyranny. Theirs was a pivotal triumph of freedom over dictatorship, of good over evil, just 75 years ago. We have our freedom because of their dedication, determination, and courage.

What will you do in the 'defining moment' that comes to each of us, sooner or later?

The story of these brave young warriors can inspire us to develop greater strength, kindness, and courage in everyday life, thus making it our "go-to" mode in crisis.

If we cultivate heroism and healing in our daily actions, then we, too, may shine.

—Thea Marshall
Editor

Robert Thomas Marshall (main author)

Robert Marshall, my father, was pulled from his graduate studies of Greek, Latin, and Ancient History at Catholic University in Washington, D.C. in 1942. He was thrust into the second-in-command role with a medical aid unit attached to the 26th Infantry Division as it fought its way across Europe in WWII, culminating at The Battle of the Bulge.

Dad had received a football scholarship to attend college, and his Johnstown, PA high school yearbook describes him as "big, brainy and brawny." Beyond these useful traits, he brought two specific strengths to his new 'job.' First, his perspective as a student of history allowed him to recognize the enormity and impact of the undertaking of which he was a part and to see the value of keeping a real-time record of the history being made. Second, his keen interest in maps enabled him to guide his unit through the turmoil, often ahead of the actual battles to be fought, identifying strategically suitable locations at which to set up Medical Aid Stations to best serve the wounded soldiers that were sure to appear.

Capt. Andrew (Andy) Dedick, M.D., was my Dad's Battalion Surgeon and commanding officer during their time in Europe. In 2004, Andy wrote to my mother about his initial meeting with my father: "... when we first met and he told me he was a Greek and Latin teacher, I wished he had been assigned to the 2nd or 3rd Battalion and not to me in the 1st. We were not together too long when I discovered I had been given the finest MAC* officer in the whole U.S. Army. He was a superior individual.... He was one of the bravest of our officers and never displayed any fear whatsoever. The men in the Aid Station had only the highest respect for him, as did I...."

His comrades' admiration for him is confirmed by Capt. Stephen J. Bury, U.S. Navy (Ret.), a military historian and my father's former student. Captain Bury researched Dad's wartime exploits for an article in the 2011 *Mount Saint Mary's Alumni Magazine*. Steve also noted: "They [Marshall's division] fought at many of the fiercest battles in Europe, including the Battle of the Bulge where the young Lieutenant Marshall was awarded the Silver Star."

Throughout the chaos of warfare, Dad had kept copious notes on his vital maps of how, when, and where he and his comrades traveled, and of what they did on a day-to-day basis.

Immediately following the cessation of hostilities, while waiting in Czechoslovakia to ship home, he compiled these records on a German typewriter that he had "liberated." A skilled writer, and possessed of a dry wit, my father's unique and timely account proved "... a great asset in documenting this level of medical support for an infantry battalion in combat ..." (as noted by Col. Richard Ginn, U.S. Army, Ret. Historian) that is now part of the United States Surgeon General's archives.

---

* Medical Administrative Corps

My parents were married for 53 years. When asked if her husband reminisced about his military service, my Mom recalls his succinct comment, "I did the job I was called to do."

Walter German (co-author)

I met Walter German only through his writing and through limited long-distance communication with his daughter Tracy and son Charlie; their kind support has allowed this narrative to be published.

I also 'knew' Walt a bit through my Dad's writing. I found him to be a gracious and generous person and wish I'd been able to meet him.

Walter hadn't planned to record the story of the medics' work and movements. Further, his duties were quite different from my father's, so he didn't have the details about geographic locales and routes that were Dad's responsibility.

Still, while waiting to ship home, Walt agreed to provide the record of their Aid Station in the final weeks of the war. He faithfully emulated my Dad's voice and easy style, filling in the chronicle after my father was blown up and evacuated.

The natural choice to complete the story would have been the replacement MAC officer. But that was not to be because, as my father wryly noted, "I never got to meet Lieutenant Adee, for he packed his bags and left immediately. I would have thought he could have relaxed, but apparently he didn't realize that the shooting was finished, and that the forward areas were just as safe as the rear."

Instead, Walt German reviewed and collaborated with my Dad to complete the account of their Yankee Division Aid Station activities.

And just as Walter German embraced history, it also touched him. Walter's daughter Tracy and son Charlie report, "Walt's service in the medical corps fueled his desire to attend medical school once he had returned to the States." In Missouri, Walter practiced medicine at Smith Glynn Callaway Clinic and at the Springfield hospitals. Among his many accomplishments, Walt delivered over 9000 babies in his 39-year medical career—the reader may have been (or know someone who was) one of those infants.

Further, Col. Richard Ginn, U.S. Army (Ret. Historian), writes that Walter's words, added to my father's narrative, are "... permanently archived with the Surgeon General's Office."

Foreword

ABOUT 400 American WWII veterans die every day.

The US Department of Veterans Affairs estimated the surviving population to be 623,653 as of 30 June 2018. That translates into a loss of approximately 25% of these warriors each year—within the next several years, there will be few of our WWII vets alive.

Whenever I speak, formally or casually, about the challenges and joys that I encountered while developing my father's WWII memoirs (*Healers and Heroes*) for publication, people reach out to tell of their relatives or ask how to research their history. We are virtually all connected to at least one person involved in WWII, whether it's through family, friends, neighbors, or other people we know.

WWII ended almost 75 years ago, yet stories from that vast, prolonged maelstrom have generated numerous popular movies, including 1942's *Casablanca*. They march on through the decades: *The Bridge Over the River Kwai*, *The Dirty Dozen*, *Patton*, *Empire of the Sun*, *Schindler's List*, *Saving Private Ryan*, *Pearl Harbor*, *Inglorious Bastards*—the list is long.

Television producers, too, found inspiration in WWII stories— *Band of Brothers*, *Winds of War*, and others captured the small-screen audience.

Readers can mine an enormous treasure trove of literature from that epic conflict—fiction, memoir, archival materials, diaries, biographies.

Author Laura Hillenbrand's 2010 *Unbroken*—the biography of Olympian Louis Zamperini's WWII struggles to survive—came to the big screen in 2014. Other recent films include *Hacksaw Ridge* (2016), *Dunkirk* (2017), *Darkest Hour* (2017) and more.

Kristin Hannah's 2015 book *Nightingale*, about WWII women in the French Resistance (with an impressive 37,000+ Amazon reviews), has been optioned for a major motion picture.

WWII was "... the biggest, baddest war in the history of mankind ..." according to Rick Atkinson (*Liberation Trilogy* author). An estimated 1.9 billion people—representing nearly every country on Earth—served, and it remains the largest conflict the planet has ever seen.

It was also the deadliest military operation in terms of total casualties. Over 60 million people were killed—about 3% of the 1940 world population, according to Wikipedia.

More than 16 million Americans served during that horrific, sprawling war. The actual voices of those that survived will soon be silenced forever.

Many WWII veterans who experienced first-hand the carnage wrought in this struggle, including my own father, long remained silent about the horrors seen, the traumas witnessed and endured.

For decades, a significant subset of the Greatest Generation was also the "Silent Generation."

As the decades passed, more veterans were willing to share their stories. We are indeed lucky that much of this valuable history has now been recorded, both in print and digitally.

Still, detailed accounts composed immediately after the war are special.

After all, what does one do when hostilities cease? There are many more troops than transport home, and you're stuck on the ground in Europe for months.

What do you do? Celebrate, reflect, brood? Probably all that, but Dad writes: "Time in Linz seemed to drag, for the aid station personnel really had little to do."

Dad also notes that they had plenty of money. His unit had "[German] Marks galore ..." to spend on "... a leather valise made to order that proved too heavy for practicality ... and shoes cobbled to our individual measurements ... and pencil sketches made from sittings and photographs, etc."

But these clearly were small diversions for men of action, now tired of war and ready to head home, their job well done.

My father, Robert Thomas Marshall, used this idle time to good purpose: he compiled a matter-of-fact account of his medical unit's day-to-day activities on a German typewriter that he'd "liberated."

Dad was wounded and evacuated toward the end the war, so he enlisted the able assistance of Staff Sgt. Walter German to fill in the narrative.

As Patrick Hinchy (Oxford University) notes, this account was written when the authors "still had pinpoint sharp memories and all their official records to hand." The contemporaneous nature and easy style of this book distinguish it from many other records of WWII.

—*Thea Marshall*
March 2019

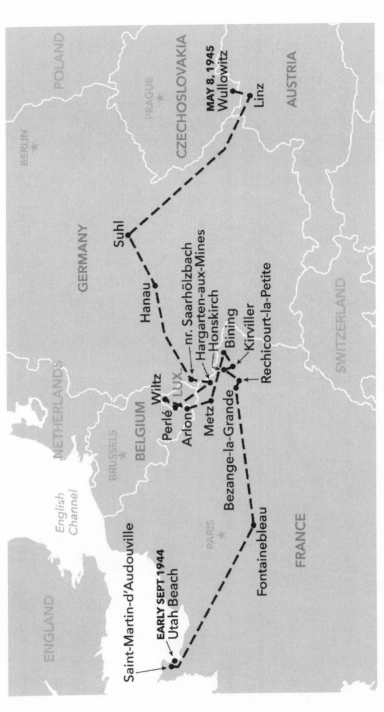

The 26th Infantry Division medics' Normandy beach landing (early September 1944) to VE Day in Czechoslovakia (May 8, 1945)

Healers and Heroes

WWII Combat Medics:
Mud and Blood from the
Normandy Beaches to
The Battle of the Bulge

Preface

HALF A CENTURY AGO a small band of young men—part of a much larger crowd—made its way across the European country-side from the Normandy coast to Czechoslovakia. We had crossed the Atlantic on a ship called the *Santa Maria* (of all things), landing on Utah Beach some months[1] after D-Day. We moved in fits and starts, and a crow would have been dizzied trying to fly over our line of march.

In fact, we did a minimum of actual marching, for being among the motorized elements, we medicos made our way in jeeps and trucks. We were the personnel of a rifle battalion aid station and as such, noncombatants, but we experienced more combat than many of the troops in the ETO.[2] This account of our day-by-day movements is naturally microcosmic, covering the actions of only a handful of men (and those with whom we came in immediate contact), but it is a tale that deserves to be told as much as many I've read covering the momentous events of those perilous years.

Our medical detachment was as solid a bunch of American citizen-soldiers as you would have found in the entire theater of operations. Most of the two dozen-odd GIs were New Englanders— after all, we were a part of the "Yankee Division."[3] The few outsiders

---

1. Marshall and his compatriots set foot on the Continent on September 7, 1944.
2. European Theater of Operations.
3. The 26th Infantry Division included the 101st, 104th, and 328th regiments, each of which included three rifle battalions. The division's nickname dates back to WWI. Before heading "over there," the commanding general assembled a group of Boston journalists and asked for suggestions for an appropriate unit appellation. One said, "Call it the 'Yankee Division,' as all New Englanders are Yankees."

Capt. Robert Thomas Marshall, Europe 1945; after hostilities.
Photo courtesy of Ann Hall Marshall.

came in for a lot of good-natured ribbing, particularly Herbie
Scheinberg, who hailed from Brooklyn. But Herbie could hold his
own with the "Bawstun mack'rel snapuhs" as he called the division.
Give and take and no morale problems.

There were, as you will see, some bona fide heroes in our
outfit, and I was not one of them. Yours truly was one of the fastest
sprinters in the Third Army—all I needed to show my stuff was
the right direction and the proper motivation. The direction was
usually west or south, since the fighting was normally east and

north. The motivation was a shell burst or two in the vicinity, or the occasional burst of machine-gun fire.

Essentially, this book was assembled and written by me, with assistance from Walter German, in the weeks immediately following the end of the fighting. The original manuscript was the output of a liberated German Army portable typewriter, both of which now sit before me. We used our own recollections, fresh as they were, as well as those of our comrades, for the basis of our story. In addition, we had a copy of the aid station casualty log, which was maintained by our clerk, Barney Menard. We also drafted a list of each location where our aid station had been set up along our route, together with the dates. Finally, we still had practically all of the detailed maps we had personally used, many of which were marked with the routes we had followed, along with some scrawled observations.

I have re-typed our original manuscript, correcting some typos and misspellings. In light of some of the opinions, conclusions, and character assessments expressed therein, I have not hesitated to add or criticize. The original manuscript may not have always reflected the respect and admiration I personally had for the aidmen and other aid station personnel, but I can assure you I had plenty. Time has only served to increase such. However, I see no reason to believe that my observations regarding the character of others was out of line, either for better or worse.

This account has two authors. Walt German picked up the story [*Editor's note:* the last two chapters] after a jeep I was riding in was blown to smithereens by a mine near Hanau, Germany, and the passengers got pretty banged up. Four of us—Al Daigle, Fred Orlovich, Denny Madden, and I—left the aid station in the jeep that day; Daigle and I were able to return, but not until after the end of the fighting.

—Robert T. Marshall
Emmitsburg, MD
September 22, 1995

Band of Young Medics
Post-hostilities, Czechoslovakia, 1945

Front row, left to right: Albert Daigle, Herbert Scheinberg, John Waryasz, Edward Geisler, George Trabucco, Samuel Melnicoff.

Back row, left to right: Milky, Martin Cohen, Angelo Nicolo, Frank Valiga, Daniel Cacchia, James Rullo, Henry Menard, Charles Touchette, Walter German.

Photo courtesy of Ann Hall Marshall.

Prologue

THE MEDICAL DETACHMENT of the 1st Battalion, 328th Infantry Regiment, 26th Infantry Division was a tiny cog in the Third Army which was, of course, led by Gen. George S. Patton, "Old Blood and Guts." We saw that legendary war-horse on only one occasion: we were going up the road and his motorcade of jeeps was going down. No messages, inspirational or otherwise, were passed along. As a matter of fact, we rarely glimpsed generals of any sort—indeed, we saw General Paul, commander of the Yankee Division, only twice.[1] Even full-bird colonels made themselves pretty scarce, so our impressions of and dealings with the higher brass were confined to the battalion COs,[2] who were majors or lieutenant colonels at most. Since these were getting shelled and shot at as much as the rest of us, they were usually pretty decent men to deal with. I should mention that two of the 328th battalion commanders were killed—Robert Servatius[3] of the 2d Battalion in the Forêt de Bride et de Koecking near Dieuze, France, and Spencer Mattingly of the 3d Battalion on the road up from Clervaux, Luxembourg.

---

1. Maj. Gen. Willard Stewart Paul. Though he received a regular Army commission in 1917, Paul never served overseas in WWI. He assumed command of the 26th Division in August 1943 and led the division through its various stateside training maneuvers and throughout its service in the ETO. Paul remained on active duty after the war (attaining the rank of lieutenant general) and after retirement served as president of Gettysburg College (1956–61).

2. Commanding officer.

3. Maj. Robert J. Servatius suffered a mortal wound during a barrage of mortar fire on November 12, 1944. He had just assumed command of the battalion the night before.

Healers and Heroes

As an assistant battalion surgeon, or to be more specific, outside man for the battalion aid station, I had one of the best jobs in the army. My immediate superior, Capt. Andy Dedick[4] (the battalion surgeon) and I got along famously. As long as we kept the flow of casualties moving steadily to the rear, nobody bothered us. The few instances to the contrary stand out because they were so rare. For example, while we were sitting in a convoy on a trail in the above-mentioned Forêt de Bride, who should come along but General Paul. He stopped long enough to give us hell because we had a Red Cross banner on the truck, which was not being used to haul casualties. We took it off, of course, but I seem to recall that it magically reappeared in a day or two, which is more than Paul ever did.

Then there was the time Col. Ben R. "Jake" Jacobs stormed into the aid station while the battalion was attacking Honskirch, wanting to know why the casualties up ahead were not getting better attention. We pointed out that some of the casualties were aid station personnel—Paul "Porky" Compagnone was killed, Frank Novicki was hit in the leg, and our jeep was demolished. I suspect it was a mortar round from Honskirch that did them in. We were not immune to the dangers of combat. I further suspect that the mortar fire in question was brought about by a bunch of 761st[5] tankers who debouched into the little clearing where this incident occurred and stoked up their cooking fires, which acted as a sort of smoke signal to the Germans in Honskirch: "Here we are, whatcha gonna do about it?"—hence the explosive reply. Anyway, Jake cooled and we continued to mop up as best we could.

---

4. Capt. Andrew P. Dedick (another non-New Englander, hailing from Pennsylvania) was awarded the Purple Heart and Bronze Star during his service with the Yankee Division.

5. This armored unit was the 761st Tank Battalion—the "Black Panthers"—a segregated African American outfit. The men of the 761st distinguished themselves in combat, earning a Medal of Honor, eleven Silver Stars, and several hundred Purple Hearts. One of the unit's officers, 1st Lt. Jack Robinson, would go on to earn fame as the legendary professional baseball player, Jackie Robinson. When the battalion joined the Third Army, Patton told the men, "I don't care what color you are as long as you go up there and kill those Kraut sonsofbitches." But in private he confessed, "They gave a good first impression, but I have no faith in the inherent fighting ability of the race."

During the Battle of the Bulge, we were fighting in the Ardennes near Arsdorf, Luxembourg, when Major Parriot came in as our new battalion CO. We were working out of the little village of Eschette, but Parriot told Captain Dedick to bring the station right up into the woods. It was very cold and snowy, and Andy politely informed the major that we couldn't handle casualties very well in the woods, but would obey the order. The major didn't want to impede us in our work; he told Andy to use his own judgment and never bothered us again after that.

When the battalion was on-line, or even being held in the regimental reserve, there was enough artillery and small arms fire to keep all but those who had pressing business out of our hair. On the other hand, we were not out in the foxholes, so our exposure was not on a 'round-the-clock basis, but was directly tied to the volume of business we received in the form of casualties. Since we were almost always able to set up in a house or barn (or the occasional *gasthaus*), our creature comforts surpassed those of the dogfaces in the line. We did our job, occasionally under fire, but the real medical heroes were the company aidmen—the combat medics who worked right alongside the riflemen.

The little, hedgerow-bound field in Normandy where HQ Company, including our aid station, made bivouac for our first month on the Continent in the fall of 1944 was a pleasant home away from home. True, some amenities were missing; for example, we were under canvas. The dogfaces—two to a pup tent—were a bit crowded, but we "brass" were allowed two shelter halves apiece,[6] so our Boy Scout apartments were quite tolerable. The weather was pleasant for the most part; a chilly evening could be offset by placing a candle in a number ten can—a nifty stove for my little tent.

---

6. A shelter—or "pup"—tent comprised two halves, with each soldier carrying one. The two buttoned together to form a complete tent to accommodate two soldiers. Its basic features had remained unchanged since the Civil War.

The head cook groused that among our mountains of equipment, no space had been allotted to a proper can opener. He actually penned a letter to the editor of the popular GI magazine, *Stars and Stripes*, in Paris and lo, a couple of days later a messenger arrived bearing a sturdy government-issue device suitable for the operations of a busy battalion kitchen!

Our respite on the bucolic French coast was the calm before the storm and, I might add, the chow was pretty good.

During this period, the line-company GIs underwent training marches, but our aid station personnel weren't required to participate. We were, for all practical purposes, gentlemen of leisure. The station itself was in one corner of a field in a command post tent[7] and business was very slow; our station log was just getting opened up. Our first half-dozen entries were all for noncombat ailments. The only one I recall was one Lt. Herman Weiss whose malady was noted as *lues*, a medical term for syphilis. Captain Dedick decided I should try my hand at giving the libidinous shavetail[8] his periodic shot of penicillin, so I positioned the needle at his bare butt and gave a gentle push. Lieutenant Weiss jumped a couple of feet in the air, howling. It was pointed out to me that the proper needle technique was a quick jab with the flick of the wrist. That was my first and last needle duty.

I also proved a failure at communicating with the locals in French. When I accosted a young boy seeking information of some sort, my Catholic high school Father Fitzgibbon French didn't work at all. The poor lad looked at me as if I were speaking Swahili.

Entertainment-wise, we had Abie Interest and his trusty motion picture projector. On a warm evening after dark, we could walk up the lane a few fields and take in a movie, lounging on the greensward. I am certain we celebrated Mass regularly

---

7. The official designation was "Tent, Fire-Resistant, Command Post, M1942, Olive Drab." This small wall tent was intended to provide working space for staff personnel. The CP tent was 7 feet wide, 11 feet 10½ inches long, and 7 feet tall at the ridge.

8. Army slang for "second lieutenant"—borrowed from the term used to describe a freshly broken pack mule.

with Father Bransfield, but not a detail of where and when comes back now.

While we cooled our heels in Normandy, the fighting was moving rapidly to the east. By this time, our boys had reached the Moselle River and were bogging down due to logistics SNAFUs. The famous Red Ball Express had been organized the previous month to speed supplies from the beaches to the front, and the Yankee Division made its contribution to the effort in men and trucks.[9] This affected our battalion not at all, although some of us were fervently hoping that we would get assigned to guard duty along the route, rather than having to deal with frontline work.

By the time October rolled around we did indeed start to move, and kept right on moving to the Pont-à-Mousson bridgehead where the 80th Division was already on line.

But I'm getting ahead of myself....

---

9. The logistics involved with supplying the twenty-eight army divisions furiously bulldozing their way across France and Belgium after D-day were daunting indeed. The so-called "Red Ball Express" was marshaled to meet the immediate demand, but actually only operated from August to November, 1944. At its peak, the Red Ball Express comprised nearly 6,000 vehicles hauling over 12,000 tons of fuel and matériel to forward depots daily.

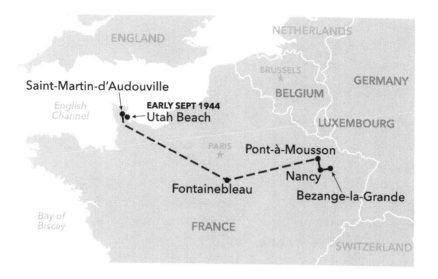

CHAPTER 1

Ready for War

THE BEGINNING OF THE chronicle of the medical detachment (two officers and twenty-odd enlisted men) of the 1st Battalion, 328th Infantry, is somewhat obscure.

It has a thousand possible beginnings—the reactivation of the regiment in '43, the coastal patrol, Camp Gordon, the Tennessee maneuvers, Fort Jackson, the staging area at Camp Shanks,[1] or the final embarkation in Brooklyn aboard the SS

---

1. Camp Shanks, the largest point of embarkation in WWII, was located in Orangetown, New York. It housed around 50,000 troops and was nicknamed "Last Stop, USA" by GIs. During the final year of the war, it was used to house German and Italian POWs.

Santa Maria. We could start with the boat trip itself, or the debarkation at Utah Beach on the Cherbourg Peninsula one rainy afternoon and evening, and the subsequent march—our welcome to France and our introduction to the infamous French mud. That night we slept in a field and the next day marched to what was to be our bivouac area for almost a month: a pasture belonging to one Monsieur Jean Gejean, adjoining the church of the quaint village of Saint-Martin-d'Audouville.

We might begin our story with the first casualties of the 26th Division, when some men accidentally set off booby traps that were still on the beaches and among the hedgerows. Or perhaps we could begin with the rainy night (yes, another rainy night) that marked our departure for the western front. It was a two-day trip at that time, which we broke with a one-night camp in a field near Fontainebleau, the suburb of Paris where Napoleon once had a summer palace, but which we will remember more for the three French prostitutes who tried to service the entire 328th Regiment. *La belle France!* These aspiring camp followers eventually *decamped* under protest, waving their health cards under the very noses of the officers who finally ran them off (Maj. "Swampy" Hilton and Capt. Andy Dedick, in case the names are of interest).

But I like to think the real story of the 1st Battalion medics began the following afternoon, October 5, 1944, in a fine mist, when we crossed the Moselle River on a span that the engineers were still working on. There we joined the bridgehead established by the 80th Division only a few days before. It was the task of the 328th Regiment to support the 80th in a holding position,[2] and thus the 1st Battalion found itself digging foxholes in a patch of woods at the western foot of a hill upon which perched the ruins of a medieval castle. On the other side of the river was the city of Pont-à-Mousson. The night passed without incident but was nevertheless memorable, for it was the first night of many the 1st Battalion was to spend within range of the enemy guns.

---

2. The 328th was attached to the 80th Division from October 2 to October 15, 1944.

In the afternoon of the next day, we moved into positions that a battalion of the 80th had prepared and held for a few days. Baker Company[3] went into the village of Morville-sur-Seille, while Able and Charlie went into the area north of that town on the west bank of the river. Battalion headquarters and the aid station were located in dugouts near the crossroads located halfway between Morville and Atton. The dugouts were excellent affairs: the engineers had built them by scooping out a large trench with a bulldozer, felling logs across the excavation, and covering them with the same dirt in the same manner. We felt very secure inside them. The men had built smaller dugouts for sleeping quarters. Once a Coleman gasoline lantern lighted the aid station, and the communications section installed a telephone on the battalion switchboard, the 1st Battalion medics were ready for war!

Not much happened in the aid station dugout. Once, a shell landed several hundred yards away and immediately became the subject of much discussion and bragging on the part of all who were around at the time. Our own artillery, which was located in the rear and whose fire was being directed from the castle, was firing intermittently, and that was the war, as far as we were concerned. If the day was pleasant, the medics would go in small groups to the battalion OP[4] that was located in a World War I pillbox in the edge of the woods facing Morville. From there we could look through field glasses toward the enemy lines, but it was more of a pastoral setting than a battlefield, to our way of thinking.

I don't think the date of October 8, 1944 would have much significance to the men of the 1st Battalion medics until nightfall, for who of us wouldn't remember our first casualty? Those nights were very dark while we were hunkered in the dugout near the crossroads, so when Captain Royds of Able Company called in to report that one of his men had been shot, nobody relished the

---

3. The author follows the common practice of referring to the alphabetical company letters by their corresponding designation in the WWII–era military phonetic alphabet: Able, Baker, Charlie, Dog, Easy, Fox, George, etc.
4. Observation post.

trip up to the company CP[5] in the pitch darkness to pick up the casualty. But in a few minutes, several of us had piled into the jeep and were off.

It was difficult to see, and we figured the route we had reconnoitered by daylight would be almost impossible to navigate since it was merely a trail through the woods. So we stuck to the road instead and went around to the left out of the battalion sector, intending to swing back to the Able CP on the same road. The plan was good, but it made no allowance for the condition of the road, and before we knew it, we were sitting in the jeep with its hind end pointing towards the heavens while the front end was deeply immersed in a shell hole in the road.

We got a couple of 3d Battalion men who were stationed nearby (who had challenged us but a few seconds before) and managed to manhandle the jeep out of the hole so we could proceed. We still had about a mile to go to get to Able Company, so from that point on, one of us walked in front of the jeep. When we were almost to the CP, we met Lt. Kermit Miller and a couple of the GIs carrying the casualty, Pvt. Robert Best. The unlucky soldier had been shot in the head by one of our own guards when he failed to give the password, having been challenged three times.

Marty Cohen, the aidman, had patched the wound up as well as possible, but Best was dead by the time we arrived. We squeamishly picked up our first combat casualty (and our first corpse), put him on a litter, loaded the litter on the jeep, and felt our way back to the aid station, taking special pains to navigate around the shell hole that had caused us grief on the way out. The entire trip had taken about three-quarters of an hour, but it seemed an eternity to those of us who had made it—and also to those back in the station, who were anxiously awaiting the next call to go out.

A hush settled over the group as we came in through the double blackout blankets into the brightly lit aid station. Captain

---

5. Command post.

Dedick checked the wound and confirmed that the casualty was dead, while the men stood about silently. Then a couple of them carried the litter and its occupant back out into the night, and one by one the 1st Battalion medics filed solemnly out of the aid station. Words were at a premium. This was war.

A day or two later, the 1st Battalion was relieved by the 3d Battalion. We moved into a reserve position about halfway between the old one and Mousson Castle. Again the aid station was situated in an engineer-constructed dugout of the same type, possibly a bit larger, and again the nights were black, possibly a bit blacker.

It was on our first night there that Evans, our mess sergeant, served his famous blackout supper. We didn't get to the area until late afternoon, so by the time the kitchen was set up and operational, it was already dark—and by the time supper was ready, it was *really* dark. The night was punctuated by the oaths of those unfortunates falling into foxholes and ditches as they groped their way to the kitchen area; it was only a hundred yards from the aid station dugout, but it might as well have been a mile. Our medics, Bruegge, Cacchia, and Watkins, stumbled about for a half hour trying to find the mess line, and ended up back at the aid station, still looking. They decided to go to bed supperless. "Jimmy the Greek," a cook, made his classic remark to one of the more impatient diners: "If you'll get your damn foot out of the pot I'll give you some potatoes, and not before!"

Most of the men had a chance to get washed up a bit while we were in this area (we stayed several days). Then one morning we packed up and set off on foot for Montauville on the west bank of the Moselle, a couple of kilometers from Pont-à-Mousson. The sun was out and, as we swung through the streets of that city and the country roads around it, we felt as if we were seasoned veterans. (We had been in the line for a week at most, and it was strictly a holding position at that.) We climbed the hill on the west side of Montauville to the assembly area. The last couple of kilometers were uphill and the going was really tough for the doughs who had been sitting around in foxholes for the past couple of weeks. We loaded as many as we could on the aid station jeep and truck, and ferried them until we came to another exhausted group sitting along the roadside; we'd unload the rested men and pick up the tired ones.

We set up the aid station in a cut in the bank along the road, near the top that overlooked the village and the valley. We backed the truck in and fastened one end of the CP tent to the end of the truck and hit the sack for the night. We didn't do much the next day. It was sunny and I remember walking to the top of the hill where the regimental aid station was set up. We saw large formations of bombers flying overhead, leaving their vapor trails across the blue sky.

The orders came down that we were to leave that night to take up position with the rest of the division, which had not come to Pont-à-Mousson with the 328th Regiment, but which had gone into the line somewhere east of Nancy. After supper we packed the station up and got the vehicles lined up with the rest of those from Headquarters Company and waited for the convoy to take off. As usual, the night was black. The trip was *almost* without incident: the medical truck had a bit of excitement when it nearly ran over the embankment, off the road, and into the valley. I forgot to mention that in the course of fraternizing in Montauville, we came close to losing two of the boys—Denny Madden and Charles Touchette—who got potted and didn't get back until the convoy was actually pulling out.

Excitement hit us in earnest when we came to Athienville after passing through Nancy. Sam Solomon had been on the advance quartering party and was there to meet us with the news that the Germans were just on the other side of the hill organizing a big counterattack. Then he showed us where to park. The boys, including the MAC[6] officer, dug with great vigor, which was even increased by the occasional landing of some enemy shells over the next hill.

---

6. Medical Administrative Corps.

As a result of the truck running off the road, Captain Dedick and boys in it didn't arrive until day was breaking. It was Sunday morning, October 15, 1944. No counterattack developed. As far as that goes, neither was there an attack itself. Our battalion exec,[7] Major Hilton, was giving us his own muddled interpretation of the enemy shells when he passed that bit of news to the quartering party. Anyhow, we dug until we were so tired that we flopped into the holes and went to sleep.

In a couple of hours, along came Maj. Gen. Willard S. Paul (the 26th division commander) in his jeep, complete with MPs and jeeps fitted with machine guns all over the place. Our medics, as well as most of the battalion, were dug in right alongside the road, so the first thing we knew Major Hilton was catching little blue hell from the general for allowing the foxholes to be dug so close together. We were all enjoying this dressing-down from a distance, for it was a bit of indirect revenge for the scare the major had given us with his false alarm earlier in the morning. Our revenge was short-lived, however, for the next thing we knew, the general had roared off in all his glory, and we were set to work digging new holes farther apart. It was a helluva way to spend a Sunday morning.

That afternoon a group of the battalion officers went forward to reconnoiter the positions we were to move into that night and the next day. We were relieving a battalion of the 101st Infantry Regiment. The trip was uneventful, but we returned just in time to see two German planes come over at treetop level strafing our troops around Athienville. It was our first experience of this sort, so everybody jumped out of their holes to see the show. This was unfortunate, for one of the boys from Mike Company, which was just down the road from us, was hit by one of our own .30-caliber machine guns, even though it was firing in antiaircraft mode. The planes themselves did no damage.

---

7. Executive officer (often abbreviated XO). Second in command (of the battalion in this case), the XO generally functioned as the supervisor of the battalion headquarters sections.

The line companies were changing that night, but we decided not to move the aid station until the next morning, as the 101st battalion aid station we were relieving would cover for us until that time. In the course of the troop shift, Lieutenant Noblette, a platoon leader, shot a GI—possibly Walter Byton of Charlie Company—through the right thigh because he failed to give the password.

The next morning, we moved up to our new home in the Forêt de Bezange-la-Grande. The 101st Regiment's medics had dug out a spot about four feet deep in which they had pitched their command post tent, so we did likewise when they left. This served as the aid station, while the men dug individual foxholes. The battalion CP was in a World War I-era pillbox a couple of hundred feet up the road. A generous layer of thick mud covered all of the ground and the road in that area. We would call this position home from the 16th to the 25th.

The tactical dispositions were of interest: We had two rifle companies dug in side by side on the northern edge of the woods, while the 3d Battalion was dug in on the northern edge of the Bois de Piamont. The thousand meters or so that separated these two woods was open ground and was not occupied to any extent. We put a couple of medics and a jeep in the Bois de Piamont each night to act as a collecting point for the company that was stationed there.

On occasion, when two patrols were going out into Moyenvic and the small patch of woods south and west of Moyenvic, we put an additional collecting point in the pillbox that Lieutenant McGeehan was using for his platoon CP. Madden, Honnaker, Waryasz[8], and I drove out in the jeep early in the evening and waited until almost midnight when both patrols reported back to McGeehan's CP, their missions accomplished and no men

---

8. On the rosters, this name is spelled both as Waryasz and Warzasz; the former spelling will be used throughout this account.

injured, then we returned to the aid station. For a change, the night was fairly light.

Editor's note: As the various elements involved in the U.S. Army's system of treating battlefield casualties are mentioned repeatedly throughout this memoir, a brief explanation is in order. Administration of this highly mobile medical service was overseen at the division level. Organizationally, each division had a medical battalion comprising a battalion headquarters, three collecting companies (designated A, B, and C), and a clearing company (D). Each collecting company included its own headquarters section, a station platoon, a litter-bearer platoon, an ambulance platoon, and a liaison section.

When a soldier was wounded in combat, he began what was called the "chain of evacuation." After receiving first aid on the scene by a combat medic, the wounded soldier was assisted to a *collecting point* to be transported, along with other casualties, to the nearest *battalion aid station*—such as the one to which the author was assigned—for stabilization; these aid stations were typically set up within a few hundred yards of the front lines. From there, casualties were rounded up by collecting company personnel and transported to *collecting stations* where they received triage. Patients with minor wounds were patched up and returned to duty; critical cases were dispatched to the *clearing station* for emergency treatment (think of a busy metropolitan ER) or a nearby *field hospital* for surgery, while the remainder were transported to an *evacuation hospital*. There was usually a chaplain on duty at each clearing station as well. The clearing station was typically set up near the medical battalion CP to centralize communication, supply, and transportation. Each "link" in this chain was progressively farther away from the front.

Our stay in the woods will also be remembered for the ersatz shower that Joe Vella built out of a barrel. Major Hilton had just gotten a new Thompson submachine gun (which he later discarded because it was too heavy to carry[9]) and its virgin task was to shoot a few holes in the bottom of the barrel to provide the shower effect.

Watkins and Walls spruced themselves out with an oversized foxhole, which they used for poker games after dark. It was big enough to hold five or six men. Bill Marranzini, an aidman with Able, was evacuated for a hernia he had developed, and Jim Kallal went up to his place. Staff Sgt. Walt German came to us from the regimental section as a replacement.

Lieutenant Koenig from Dog Company provided us with excitement one night when his men shot a Serbian in the rear end, then captured him and hauled him into the aid station—our first prisoner! It turned out the poor sod was only a stable helper for the Germans.

Koenig also provided us with a minor flurry when his men shot a Frenchman who was coming between the lines. The gentleman died as a result of the wound, but Major Hilton got it into his head that the body should be removed and that the medics were the logical ones to remove it. A big squawk went up from the medicos, the result being that Major Hilton and Andy went out to do the job. This they accomplished by tying the corpse's hands together and the feet likewise, slipping a pole through, and placing the pole on their shoulders, just like victorious hunters returning from the kill.

On October 25, we pulled out of these positions into an assembly area in another patch of woods south of Bezange-la-Grande. Nothing happened here, so after having spent the night in tents, we entrucked the next morning and took a circuitous route to another area in a draw 1,200 meters northeast of the village of Bures. As we came into this place we met elements of

9. The illustrious .45-caliber M1928A1 (later models were designated the M1 and M1A1) Thompson submachine gun—better known as the "Tommy gun"—tipped the scales at over 10.5 lbs. empty.

the 104th Regiment (which we were relieving) withdrawing. They had had a rough time taking the area just up ahead, as the men and terrain showed. I well remember a stack of bloody litters that their aid station had left behind when it pulled out. The 328th was taking over this area that the 104th had won, but our 1st Battalion was being held in the regimental reserve, so we had nothing to do but wait for the next couple of days.

There was nothing out of the ordinary about our area. With his usual thoughtfulness, Captain Miller, the S-1,[10] had parked the medics in the bottom of the draw through which ran a small stream. This was very handy, for any foxhole that we dug over a foot deep was certain to have running water seeping through from the creek in an hour or so. I circumvented the captain by digging only a shallow hole, then building up all around it with square pieces of sod to the height of a couple of feet. Over this I pitched my shelter halves and thus had a very snazzy home. The aid station we did not bother to dig in, but merely pitched the two command post tents end to end.

I well remember a poker game in my sod dugout one evening after dark. Andy, Lt. Tony Geydos, Lt. Dean Sauders, another officer, and I were busily exchanging our francs when the Heinies favored us with an artillery serenade. Actually they must have been targeting our 263d Artillery, which was set up a couple of hundred yards east of us, for it would have been impossible for them to drop any shells in our immediate area, what with a goodly sized hill rising sharply between us and them. However, the shells still had to whistle over our heads, and the game came to an abrupt stop as the gamesters struggled vainly for choice positions on the bottom of the dogpile. I remember it especially well, for in spite of the fact that it was *my* dugout, I ended up on top of the pile holding a can of stale urine, which we had not had time to dispose of.

---

10. S-1 is the designation for the administration and personnel section of the headquarters detachment. The officer in charge of this section (who also functioned as the battalion adjutant) was generally referred to as "the S-1."

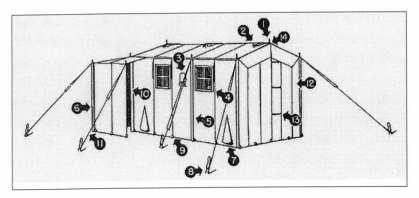

A contemporary illustration of a typical Command Post (CP) tent from WWII ETO — "Tent, Fire-Resistant, Command Post, M-1942, Olive Drab, Stock No. 24-T-318-33" — showing: 1) Spindle (2) Ventilator Ridge (3) Communication Pocket Flap (4) Window Sash (5) Upright Pole (6) Upright Pole (7) Side Ventilator Duct (8) Pin (9) Foot Stop Line (10) Entry (11) Eave Line (12) Extension Cloth (13) Door Fastener (14) Upright Pole. Photo, public domain, provided courtesy of Aden Nichols.

The duffle bags were brought up from a warehouse in Nancy at this time and we were treated to a dinner of French roast beef after Major Hilton killed a cow with three .45 slugs and two blows from an axe.

Father Bransfield said Mass on the 29th, and I remember thinking at the time that the brevity of the sermon must have been somehow connected with the occasional Heinie shells that sailed overhead. Chaplain McClung was busy taking orders for clothes he was picking up from the QM[11] store in Toul, while Lt. Fred Warrick was sporting a Luger that he'd acquired (nobody knows where), the first souvenir of this kind that I had seen. I remember his wanting the chaplain to hold it for him in case he should be captured by the enemy, who, we heard, took a dim view of Americans carrying German weapons.

---

11. Quartermaster.

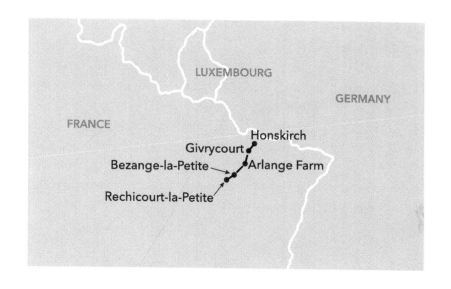

CHAPTER 2

How a Jew Helped a Nazi

AT THIS TIME, the regimental aid station was set up only a mile or so behind us on the road leading out of Bures. The crew had dug themselves into the side of the hill, and I know this was the first and last occasion on which they soiled their lily-white hands by digging foxholes. (In all fairness, we soon broke ourselves of the habit as well.) Lieutenant Markham was one of our few casualties when a chunk of masonry dented his scalp during some excitement in the town of Coincourt, where Charlie Company was holding court.

From this area we moved into Rechicourt[1] to relieve the 2d Battalion. This was on November 1, and from the moment we landed, things began to happen. "Coke"[2] and I spent the best part of the day reconnoitering the companies' positions. Able Company was to take over the southwest slope of Hill 264 and Baker the southwest slope of Hill 253; the Heinies provided occupation forces for the other sides of these respective mounds, while the hilltops made a suitable no-man's land.

The enemy was also in Bezange-la-Petite. That day was foggy, so we had no trouble contacting Lieutenant Lehrman of Fox Company and Captain Carrier of George Company, which Baker and Able were relieving respectively. The route to Able would be good: a straight road almost to the company CP. However, the one to Baker involved a bit of cross-country work as well as a good sense of direction. The line companies were not to make the switch until after dark, but we made the aid station swap in the afternoon. We had a couple of downstairs rooms for the station, while the gang slept in the attached barn.

The fireworks started shortly after dark when George Company, which had not yet been relieved, called to say they had a couple of casualties. We went out to find Lieutenant Randazzize (who had been in charge of the officers' mess at Fort Jackson) shot through the ankle, as well as a couple of enlisted men who were even worse off.

We had gone at first to the George Company CP, but they had not only failed to furnish us guides to (or at least a faint idea of) where the casualties were, they also had moved one of the wounded from the spot where he was hit (fairly close to the evacuation route we had planned) to their own ammo dump, which

---

1. Réchicourt-la-Petite.
2. Presumably S. Sgt. Daniel Cocomazzi.

was quite a piece out of the way. I naturally blew my stack, but we finally wandered all over the damn hill and got everybody collected and started back. During the whole trip back, the least injured of the three was hollering like a stuck pig, until I felt sure the Heinies up the road thought Ringling Brothers' circus was headed for Bezange-la-Petite. Somehow we managed to get back without drawing any enemy (or friendly) fire.

The next night we got a call from Able and went out to find that a shell had landed in T/4 Joe Cabral's foxhole. He was one of the aidmen with Able. We dug him out and brought him back to the aid station, but he was dead when we got there (and probably had been when we picked him up). Friday night T/4 Bill Market, a Baker aidman, got a shell fragment in his scalp, so we drove out and picked him up. Larry Honaker from the station went out to Baker as a replacement.

During the time we were at Rechicourt until the attack on November 8, a few odds and ends cropped up to keep us amused. Father Bransfield was staying with us and celebrated Mass each morning in the sacristy of the village church. Indeed, the sacristy was about all that was left of the church. Andy and I went out to pay a social call to Baker Company, and spent most of the trip hitting the dirt when a machine gun opened up nearby. We later discovered that it was a Dog Company gun firing from Hill 296 over our heads into Bezange.

Organizing himself into a one-man commando unit, Maj. Swampy Hilton went out to blow up a German artillery piece that stood between the lines in Baker Company's sector. He came back and gave a glowing report of the success of this mission—how he had crept under the very noses of the Germans, tied dynamite on the gun, lit it, crept back, and watched the gun blow sky high. We later learned that the gun had already been deactivated by the 2d Battalion, while Honaker, who was an eyewitness, told us that Swampy had confined his efforts to throwing hand grenades at the offending weapon from a foxhole within the safety of our own lines.

Morgan Madden and Herbie Scheinberg were given the task of closing the latrine in our backyard and digging a new one, but they got confused, reversed the order, and dug the new one first. It was lucky for them that they did it thus, for whilst they were digging, a mortar shell dropped squarely into the old latrine and obliterated it. The odd part was that neither was injured, although they were within fifteen feet of the explosion. Rechicourt also saw me—after two long, hard, and faithful years—shed golden bars for those wrought of silver.[3] For a while I had gotten to thinking that the damn War Department had decided to let me remain a second louie for the duration as an awful example to our drafted citizenry not to go to OCS,[4] especially not MAC OCS.

One dark night, Lt. George Winecoff, exec of Baker, came into the aid station humbly seeking our assistance. It seems he was unable to navigate his usual ration route to the company and wanted us to guide him over the one we were using for evacuation—the route we had figured out all for ourselves, and that was a much better one. It tickled us to think that the infantry should come seeking such technical help from the medics whom they usually razzed for knowing so little of such matters. But we pitched in and delivered the rations and kept the gloating to a minimum.

Finally on the morning of November 8, the 1st Battalion attacked Bezange-la-Petite, which was our small part in the larger picture, the big Lorraine offensive by Patton's Third Army[5]. The medic plan had been figured out long in advance: We would evacuate Able right from Rechicourt and would set up an alternate aid station in the Chapelle St. Pierre, which was only a short distance behind the Baker CP, directly on our route of evacuation. Before

---

3. Though gold is generally thought to be the more precious metal, in this case, silver indicated a promotion from second lieutenant to first—no more "butter bar"!

4. Officer Candidate School.

5. This attack was part of a major assault—Operation Madison—on a fifty-mile front involving the 26th, 35th, and 80th Infantry Divisions of XII Corps; the 4th and 6th Armored Divisions joined the assault later in the day.

daylight on the 8th, Bruegge, Madden, Jenkins, Geisler, German, Scheinberg, and I (along with one or two more) made our way to the chapel. We listened to the artillery preparation and watched the tracer shells from Geydos' 57-mm anti-tank guns[6] sailing through the dawn into Bezange.

The Heinies retaliated in kind, landing several shells within ten feet of the chapel and dropping a portion of its roof on Madden's head, thus giving him his first Purple Heart. But we had gotten our signals crossed and were busily praying to St. Joseph, in whose honor we mistakenly thought the chapel was erected[7]. The saints must have smiled tolerantly at our ignorance and pitched in together to give us a hand, for Madden's scratch was the only one during the counter fire.

Soon the day had come in earnest, and with it the casualties started pouring in. Baker Company's task was merely to clear the Jerries from the other side of Hill 253 and this they accomplished in short order and with a minimum of trouble after the artillery barrage had lifted. The enemy left as many dead and wounded as he had inflicted. We ran the jeep forward to the creek that flowed near the base of the hill and hand-carried the casualties down the hill. Back in the chapel, Bruegge and Geisler were busy passing out plasma and splinting, while the rest of us made it our job to bring them the patients. Lt. Joe Senger, our S-4,[8] dropped in for a visit and was soon put to work hauling wounded from the chapel back to the main aid station.

The trip from the hill wasn't too bad until the Heinies decided to blast Baker from its heights with artillery. A good many shells would just miss the top and would keep on going down into the valley near the stream straddling our evacuation route. Several

6. The 57-mm Gun M1 was an American-made variant of the British Mk II Ordnance Quick-Firing 6-pounder. Primarily an anti-tank gun, by this time the M1 was being supplied with HE (high explosive) ammunition, which made it a formidable antipersonnel weapon.

7. Many years later, Robert Marshall wrote this story out in greater detail as "Incident at Bezange-la-Petite." See www.healersandheroes.com.

8. S-4 is the designation of the logistics section of the battalion headquarters. As with all of the staff sections, the officer in command is also called "the S-4."

shells breezed in as we were getting the last of the GI casualties off the hill. One of these chaps had trench foot and exhaustion so bad that two of the boys were carrying him. We hit the dirt, waited for a breathing spell, and then lit out on the double for the jeep before more shells landed. And who should be leading our pack but the crippled exhaustion case—and he beat us all with his shell-inspired sprinting.

Next we turned to the German casualties. It would have done the Jewbaiting Nazi politicians a world of moral good to see Herbie Scheinberg helping one of their fallen warriors across the be-shelled valley floor to the chapel. Indeed, Herbie picked up a hunk of German shrapnel in his arm from a near hit during one of these excursions. It wasn't serious and Herbie kept going, but I still like to think about how I once saw a Jew earn a Purple Heart helping save Nazi lives. That's one for the books!

CHAPTER 3

Medal of Honor

OVER IN ABLE COMPANY, where the mission was to secure Hill 264 as well as Bezange-la-Petite, Coke and his boys had their hands full. Charlie Company came up in between Able and Baker through the vineyard and also joined the fracas. To add to the excitement in Rechicourt, the African American tankers of the 761st, who were supposed to charge up the road into Bezange, got mixed up somewhere along the line and came charging into Rechicourt with all guns blazing. Miracles can happen, for not a single GI was injured in this maneuver. They were finally made cognizant of their error before they could do too much damage. While mustering out at Indiantown Gap after the war, I happened to meet an officer who claimed he had been with that tank battalion that morning. According to this man, Colonel Jake had given the tankers a bum steer.

Instead of Bezange, Lieutenant Hicks of Able led his men by mistake into Lezey, where he and his sergeant were both wounded. The rest of the men got back, leaving those two behind. A bullet caught Lieutenant McGeehan squarely in the forehead. Later in the afternoon a shell, either artillery or mortar, lit near the little graveyard where Captain Kixmiller was talking to Lieutenant Swan, T/5 Alfred Wilson, and a couple of other men. Swan and one of the men were killed outright, Kixmiller was unscathed, the others wounded.

Kixmiller noticed that Wilson was a medic and told him to go over and tend to the wounded men. Without a word Wilson did just that, patching up one badly wounded man so well that Jenkins was able to get him back to the aid station alive. It was then that Kixmiller noticed that Wilson himself was hit—one leg was practically torn off and he had bad holes in the other leg and an arm. About that time, we came along the vineyard draw and evacuated him. It took us almost an hour to wade through the thick mud to the road where we got Wilson on a vehicle, so it was dark by the time he arrived at the aid station.

Editor's note: In 1995, Marshall added this postscript to the story: "Wilson died there at the aid station shortly afterwards, but I see that he is not forgotten, for only the other day the *Stars and Stripes* had an article announcing that T/5 Alfred L. Wilson had been posthumously awarded the Congressional Medal of Honor for his heroism there by the cemetery outside of Bezange." This was the only Medal of Honor awarded to a member of the 26th Division in World War II. Wilson's official award citation reads:

> [Wilson] volunteered to assist as an aidman for a company other than his own, which was suffering casualties from constant artillery fire. He administered to the wounded and returned to his own company when a shellburst injured a number of its men. While treating his comrades he was seriously wounded, but refused to be evacuated by litter bearers sent to relieve him. In spite of great pain and loss of blood, he continued to administer first aid until he was too weak to stand. Crawling from one patient to another, he continued his work until excessive loss of blood prevented him from moving. He then verbally directed unskilled enlisted men in continuing the first aid for the wounded. Still refusing assistance himself, he remained to instruct others in dressing the wounds of his comrades until he was unable

to speak above a whisper and finally lapsed into unconsciousness. The effects of his injury later caused his death. By steadfastly remaining at the scene without regard for his own safety, Cpl. [T/5] Wilson through distinguished devotion to duty and personal sacrifice helped to save the lives of at least ten wounded men.

That night Lieutenant Morales, a machine gunner with Dog Company was brought in; he had been hit by a sniper in Bezange. After dark, a cavalry group[1] began to effect the relief of the 1st Battalion. Some of the companies stayed right in Rechicourt, but at least one pulled back to Vaudrecourt farm. Still, the medics' work was not done. The next day Swampy came into the aid station to announce that he was leading a group of the A & P platoon[2] into Bezange to pick up wounded. The exact status of Bezange was something of a question at the time, but somewhere he had heard a rumor that there were wounded GIs there.

The medics were touched to the quick by this seeming slur on their work, so Trabucco, Jenkins, Couture (HQ Company supply sergeant who was helping us), and I piled in the jeep and headed for Bezange, passing by what had been Baker Company's old CP. We drove cautiously into the town. The first thing that caught our eye was a Heinie aid station, complete with Heinies. We didn't know whether to run or not, but since we were so close and didn't stand much of a chance in case they did decide to shoot, we kept on going. They proved quite friendly. There were about a dozen of them. Of course we assumed they were medics, but later found that they were the snipers who had been causing

---

1. The 2d Cavalry Group.
2. Ammunition and pioneer platoon. The A & P platoon was responsible for hauling ammunition to forward positions. The "pioneer" aspect of its job involved laying and removing mines, stringing barbed wired, and clearing obstacles (demolitions). The platoon was attached to the headquarters company and commanded by a second lieutenant with a sergeant and driver for a platoon truck armed with a .50-caliber heavy machine gun. Each of its three eight-man squads was led by a sergeant.

so much trouble. They were loading a horse cart with about six of their own wounded and some signal equipment.

I asked the *oberfeldwebel*[3] in charge if he would lend me a couple of his men to pick up our own wounded, for I felt that the presence of some Germans in our little party would be insurance against getting fired on by any other Germans who might be hanging around. He agreed and we scoured the town, but found only two GI wounded. We headed out on the road towards Lezey where Lieutenant Hicks was, but after seeing that his location was beyond our lines, we opted for discretion rather than valor. We also ran across five or six cavalrymen hiding in a barn. They were some of the troops whose job it was to relieve us; they had come into Bezange the night before but not knowing the score, they had decided to lie low, assessing the situation.

The payoff came as we were about to leave town. Along came the A & P platoon in its best battle formation, a file down either side of the main street, all with their rifles at the ready. Lieutenant Williams was walking point while Major Swampy with his submachine gun was discreetly bringing up the *rear*. We loaded the GIs on the jeep, whereupon Swampy volunteered to *lead* it back to Rechicourt and set out at once. We borrowed a couple of riflemen for guards and took off with the Heinies and their wagonload of wounded following along in the jeep's tracks.

We got back to Rechicourt at noon and at once began packing up the station to follow the rest of the battalion to Vaudrecourt farm. When we were ready to leave, Andy decided to take one last shot at grabbing Lieutenant Hicks. Along with Watkins, Jenkins, and Madden, he set off while the rest of us headed for the farm. Andy quickly realized it would be foolish to risk any more lives trying to break through to Hicks, who was probably dead by that time. We never did find out what happened to him, although the sergeant who had been with him managed to low-crawl back. Lieutenant Woods was also killed in this attack.

---

3. A German noncommissioned officer.

CHAPTER 4

Body Parts

AT VAUDRECOURT FARM we licked our wounds and rested. Wary-asz was evacuated with a high fever and Lt. Kermit Miller of Able with trench foot. On November 9, we spent the night in the hayloft of the farm and stayed all next day. Madden and Bruegge had liberated a large wall clock in Rechicourt and, after much futile discussion about the possibility of sending it home or carrying it along, jettisoned it. That night after dark, we packed up the station and set off once more in battalion convoy. Our destination was somewhere on the other side of the Seille River.

It was a helluva trip! Paul "Porky" Compagnone was driving our truck following one of the anti-tank guns. We weren't using blackout lights and I spent my time between praying and wondering whether we would end up in the ditch or with the barrel of the AT gun poked halfway through our truck and its occupants. Somehow neither happened. We passed through Vic-sur-Seille where Andy and the jeep got separated from the convoy. We finally stopped in the early hours of the next morning in an apple orchard just outside of Vic and hit the sack. We didn't set up the aid station, but we should have, as we had a couple of SIWs[1] before the morning was out.

By noon we were on the road again, stopping for the night in the woods about halfway between Morville-lès-Vic and Hampont.

---

1. Self-inflicted wound.

It was here that we lost our faith in foxholes, for some enemy shells coming in from Marsal burst in the trees and caught four men from Charlie, though they had taken cover in their foxholes. From then on, Captain Dedick announced, two thicknesses of canvas would be plenty of protection for him.

The next day we set off in our first snowfall (a herald of the bitter winter to come) and stopped for the night alongside the road leading southwest from Hampont, about 1,500 meters from that city. The night did not pass without incident, but we got off to a good start with a substantial meal. Lt. Joe Senger, Lt. Dean Sanders, Lt. Tony Geydos, Andy, and I whipped up a wonderful concoction of C ration beans, stew, and hash, into which we cut up a couple of cans of K ration cheese. We heated the stuff over a Coleman stove and went to work. After such a cold, wet day, it really hit the spot. In the middle of the night one of the other regiment's trucks turned over down the road a piece, and we sent the ambulance down to pick the injured up. Still later, a guy came looking for help, not realizing we'd already sent aid. Because no one jumped up enthusiastically to repeat the dash down the road, this messenger proceeded to tell us what he thought of the medics and our slovenly ways. Andy blew his top, but others sweetly explained that we'd already taken action.

The next morning a hand grenade went off by accident in one of the GI's pockets. He was right across the road from the aid station, and Andy was there in nothing flat, but the man died anyway.

Once more we packed up the station and set off toward the east. We stopped after a couple of kilometers across the road from an advanced collecting point of the 2d Battalion. They had already made contact farther ahead, and our own troops were working their way forward to that area. Everything was pretty much confused, so we just sat around marking time.

It was then that General Paul made another one of his infrequent visits to the battalion. He came roaring up in all his glory.

Note the troops' use of white bedsheets as camouflage in the snow. Photo, public domain, provided by the Battle of the Bulge Association (BOBA).

Practically the entire division was involved in the state of confusion that was evident in those parts, what with our finally catching up to the enemy compounded by the transportation problem that the muddy trails presented. In spite of all that, the general spent the better part of his visit giving us medics hell for having a Geneva Red Cross flag on the truck, which was not being used to haul casualties at that particular moment.

After that we moved a couple more kilometers along the same road until we came to a clearing, in the middle of which stood Berange farm. The battalion CP, Able Company, and the medics stopped in the woods on the edge of the clearing, while Jenkins and I went forward to see what the farm looked like and what sort of aid station it would make. On the way, we ran across Jefferson L. Streepey, the 2d Battalion surgeon, who was busily at work earning his Silver Star award by assiduously avoiding, by means of his foxhole, the occasional shells. The farm proved to be just what we were looking for, so we started back (by a different route because of sniper trouble) to fetch the station and bring it up.

In the meantime, all was not quiet back in the woods. The Heinies were dropping barrages on the very spot where we had left the convoy, so Jenkins and I decided to postpone our return until the shelling stopped. All hell must have broken loose in that spot, for when we did get there, there were wounded and dead all over the place.[2] Everybody had pulled back a couple hundred meters into the woods along the road, and it was there that we found them. Andy and Joe Senger and the medics had their hands full trying to take care of everyone.

Our most famous casualty of that time was Major Hilton. He had been near a burst and received its concussion and a few tiny bits of steel in his hide. He was lying there moaning and groaning, but had sufficient presence of mind to make the requisite hero's speech: "Don't bother with me, tend to the men." And seeing that he wasn't seriously wounded, Andy did just that, leaving the good major apparently quite surprised and hurt to think that his heroic statement should be taken literally.

Incidentally, this is where we picked up our extra jeep. Coke "borrowed" it from the 101st Regiment and we never returned it.

By now afternoon was well on its way. We received word that Charlie Company, which had been moving ahead through the woods on the other side of Berange farm, had casualties, so I grabbed Herbie Scheinberg and a couple other men and we set off in the jeep. We were supposed to have a guide meet us along the road but we missed the connection, so we took off on our own up the main trail. We bumped into the 2d Battalion CP, where we were warned to take it easy going any farther up the road, as the Krauts were not far off. Still no Charlie Company and nobody who seemed to know where they were, so we did a to-the-rear march and were starting back when who should come along but Lieutenant Kuligowski of

---

2. Colonel Jacobs was also wounded during this action, which occurred on November 12.

Charlie, and he was looking for us. He offered to guide us and we accepted—an almost fatal mistake, for Kuligowski's sense of direction was nonexistent.

We went for about two kilometers over hill and dale through the woods, but still no Charlie. Kuligowski was all for continuing, but he finally confessed that he didn't know where he was. (We later discovered that our farthest point of advance was behind the German lines at that time.) I blew my stack and we set off for the rear. This time we bumped into Captain Maccione, Charlie Company's CO, who promised to take us personally to his company and the casualties. We set off in a different direction entirely, and after another couple of kilometers arrived at the spot at dark. It was pitch black by the time we rounded up the casualties and were ready to start back, so we navigated through the woods by means of a compass, the first and only time I used the gadget in the ETO.

When we got through the woods, we decided to go to the farm, rather than try to find our own installation. We had a good idea that the 2d Battalion aid station would be in the farm, and it was. We unloaded the casualties, had something to eat, shot the bull awhile, and then hit the hay.

I recall talking to Lieutenant Rosebault, 2d Battalion motor officer, who was helping their medics out at the time. He told me Major Servatius had been killed and gave me the major's .45[3] when he heard I was looking for one. I felt the need for a sidearm as I never wore my Red Cross armband, and it would have been little protection and consolation had we run into trouble on the expedition just completed. Hitting the hay (literally!) was really sweet that night. I climbed up into the hayloft, undressed completely, dug a hole for myself in the hay, and burrowed in until only my nose was sticking out.

3. The M1911A1 .45-caliber semiautomatic pistol was the standard sidearm carried by commissioned officers and "mounted" troops (vehicle crews). The venerable—and powerful—1911A1 continued to be the government-issue sidearm until 1986.

The next morning we went back to the woods to find that Dedick had had twenty-two guests in the tent for the night and all of them looked miserable in dawn's early light. We packed up the station and moved to the farm. This day, Captain Royds, CO of Able Company, and Lieutenant Clothier of Baker were killed in the woods by small-arms fire. Lieutenant Lehrman of Easy Company also got it at this time. In the aid station we were busy with trench foot and exhaustion, much more so than with actual battle wounds. At one point, the number was so great that we were sending them back to the collecting company in trucks because the ambulances couldn't handle the volume.

A couple of Heinie wounded were brought to the farm. One was in great pain with lacerations of the face and eyes. We asked him if he would tell us the location of the machine guns that were causing all the trouble and he refused. Andy told him we'd have to defer medical treatment until he felt more like talking, whereupon the information really started to flow. It turned out he spoke passable English. We spoke to the S-2,[4] Captain Mumme, about this prisoner's talking, but he seemed too busy at the time to bother with such paltry information (which was the cause of no little peeve on our part).

As a result of all our evacuees, as well as those of the 2d Battalion aid station that was also located at the farm, we had an enormous salvage pile of weapons and clothing outside. The infantrymen who were going back to duty or merely passing through would often stop and sort through the stuff, looking for rubber overshoes, which were very scarce. One such group was having a field day, until one of the men picked up a likely looking overshoe and found a foot inside, whereupon all departed looking rather green around the gills. The medics had long since been hardened to such stuff—it was never a matter for much concern.

---

4. S-2 is the designation of the intelligence section of the headquarters detachment (added to the medical battalion headquarters in 1944). Its primary task involved collecting data on enemy strength and movements, and interrogating prisoners.

CHAPTER 5

Fighting Alongside the Black Panthers

IN ANOTHER COUPLE of days we were on the move again, this time to Arlange farm, about four kilometers east of our present position. This was a more elaborate arrangement, as the farm was a big place. We set up in the chapel adjoining the house. We had a job getting it cleaned up, for a rifle company had been there before us and had filled the place with straw, dirt, and trash, as well as the remains of a fire that they had built in the middle of the floor. Father Bransfield was in twice during the course of our several days there to say Mass.

We didn't have too many customers at the Arlange station, though Charles Touchette was hit in the leg one evening as he was driving the jeep around the crossroads to the north of the farm. He was evacuated the next day.

During our brief stay, we had little trouble with artillery, as the chapel was situated close to the foot of a fairly steep hill that stood between it and Dieuze (from whence the enemy fire was coming).

The line companies were posted on the top of the hill and on the down slope facing Dieuze, acting as protection for the division flank. They were all reduced by trench foot and wounds to forty or fifty men apiece, and were in lousy shape to do much fighting. It was at this place that we received our replacements, both riflemen and aidmen.[1]

The distance from the companies to the chapel aid station was only five or six hundred meters as the crow flies, but when making the trip by the road, it was four or five times as long. So the medics went to work the day after we got there and did a bit of pioneering. We cut a road through the underbrush directly up the hill. Now we were connected to the road up on top that ran behind the companies on line, parallel to the front. This proved to be well worth the effort, for when we got a call one night that some mortar shells had caught a bunch of men out of their holes at chow time, we were up and had them back in the aid station in a matter of minutes. Later, Morgan Madden and I did some target practice with our .45s.

Tuesday morning, November 21, we loaded up and started out after the Heinies who were generally withdrawing. We moved about fifteen kilometers in an easterly direction, winding up in mid-afternoon in the village of Guinzeling, where we were to relieve a battalion of the 101st Regiment.

The following morning we moved up to the next town, Lohr, where we set up shop in the village rectory, much to the dismay of the good padre, who—in one of his more explosive moments— declared that we were like beasts, compared to the German soldiery. He burst out in tears when the boys moved into his sitting room to sleep. Again, in a moment of confidence, he told me that he had once been invited by the bishop of Denver to come to that diocese, but that his parents had talked him out of it.

The troops had moved up to still another village, Insviller, but they withdrew later that night for fear of being cut off by the water, which was rising between the two places as the result of

---

1. The stubborn German defense of Dieuze resulted in many casualties, but the unforgiving weather proved to be an equally vicious foe. Slogging through the muddy forests resulted in high casualty rates—more than five hundred were evacuated from the 328th Regiment suffering from exposure and trench foot during the first four days of the operation.

the Heinies having monkeyed with some dams upstream.[2] We made one trip to Insviller, more for the sightseeing than anything else, and got the jeep stuck in a shell hole in the middle of the road around dusk. "Red" Framton and Lieutenant Warrick came up in the maintenance truck and yanked it out after dark.

Joe Vella lifted a wristwatch from the rectory and I took a Bible, but as Joe contended, they must have been jinxed, for the watch never kept good time, and I lost the Bible later on when I was evac'ed at Grossauheim. I think the good priest was more than happy when we pulled out the next morning.

We backtracked into Guinzeling and headed north to Torcheville where we selected a barn as the scene of our next endeavors. Meanwhile, the troops moved east into the woods between there and Munster. The 2d Battalion had its hands full trying to take this place but finally did. In Munster, we loaded up on ginger ale and assorted soft drinks from a local factory—the spoils of war! Friday saw us celebrating a belated Thanksgiving with turkey and all the trimmings.

Sunday morning, we moved through Munster to Givrycourt and again set up the aid station in a barn. The troops kept going north through Givrycourt for a couple of kilometers, then turned east to assault Honskirch. I remember the attack plan quite well: with Able on the left and Charlie on the right, we were to advance to the high ground just west of the city while Baker moved along the road from Vittersbourg to the town to capture it.

It was a good plan, but the Germans had other ideas. The first day saw exactly nothing accomplished. The 761st Tank Battalion— the "Black Panthers"—which was to support Baker Company, had

---

2. Actually, it was Allied airpower—more specifically, two P-47 fighter-bomber squadrons from the 362d Fighter Group—that destroyed the Etang de Lindre Dam near Dieuze as a preemptive stratagem. The dam strike and resulting flood isolated German units prior to the Third Army's advance, while preventing the enemy from releasing the water at an inopportune moment during the Allied attack. Rainfall during this period was inordinately high (the worst in twenty years), and the Moselle River flooded its banks twice.

over half a dozen medium tanks[3] knocked out and abandoned, due to mines and eighty-eights.[4] Baker suffered casualties along with the tankers, but these had to be handled by the 3d Battalion aid station in Vittersbourg.

Monday we started out again, and while the troops got a little closer this time, Honskirch was still not ours at the end of the day when the order came to withdraw under cover of smoke. We never did take the town, as we were relieved that night by the 2d Battalion, which walked in the following day unopposed.

Honskirch was a highlight for the 1st Battalion medics. We had our hands full and then some. The road out of Givrycourt to Vittersbourg was nothing but mud, and the jeeps were continually getting stuck. We had a stream of casualties the entire time we were there.

Sunday an artillery barrage caught some of the gang just by the clearing in the woods where Dog Company's mortars were set up. It killed Porky Compagnone, broke Frank Novicki's leg, and shook up Coke, Trabucco, and Bill Walls. Coke had to be evacuated the next day. The first night, Morgan Madden and I were in a jeep collecting casualties, out in the open space between the woods and Honskirch, and we didn't draw a shot. Captain Willoughby (who had assumed command of Able Company from Harry Doyle, who had gone to the rear with a

---

3. The justly famous Sherman tank—technically, the "Medium Tank, M4"—appeared in many variants. By late 1944, the M4A1 was being supplanted by the M4A3 version that touted a more powerful engine; some models were fitted with a105-mm howitzer in place of the earlier 75-mm or high-velocity 76-mm main gun. Nazi biographer Albert Speer said of the M4: "The Sherman climbs mountains our tank experts consider inaccessible to tanks. One great advantage is that the Sherman has a very powerful motor in proportion to its weight. Its cross-country mobility on level ground is, as the 26th Panzer Division reports, definitely superior to that of our tanks."

4. The German Flak 88 (which fired an 88-mm shell) was known to GIs simply as the "eighty-eight." Initially designed as an antiaircraft gun, the eighty-eight was famous for its punch and versatility: it was also employed as an antiarmor weapon as well as serving as the primary armament of the Tiger I heavy tank. The "flak" designation was derived from the German *Flugabwehrkanone* ("aircraft defense cannon") and was commandeered as the English descriptor for antiaircraft fire in general. The Germans called the gun the *acht-acht*, which made its way into English as "ack-ack."

fever the day before) was wounded and captured in the assault on Honskirch.

Monday was a repetition of Sunday. Late in the afternoon we took some of the anti-tank men out to Sainte-Élisabeth farm where we established a collecting point for Charlie Company. It was a long haul from the hill where Charlie had been fighting back to the farm. From there we still had to carry the patients back almost to Givrycourt because the road was impassible. The companies had thoughtfully withdrawn at just about dusk, leaving their wounded behind them, so we had not only the physical exertion of the job to contend with, but also the unsettling knowledge that we were working more than a mile out in front of our own outposts.

Fortunately, the Heinies didn't bother us at all, because as we later found out, they were too busy withdrawing as well. Not only did our GIs leave their wounded behind when they withdrew, but they also abandoned their heavy machine guns. So Roy Taylor, Dog Company's exec, was busy trying to get them out. Lt. Fred Warrick, the motor officer, was helping move the casualties from the farm to the aid station. Captain Kixmiller, the battalion exec, was helping clear the fields to the north.

Colonel Jacobs' driver was killed in the same area where Porky had been hit and at about the same time. Cheney, the Dog Company lieutenant who abandoned the guns (and the position, for that matter), was placed under arrest.

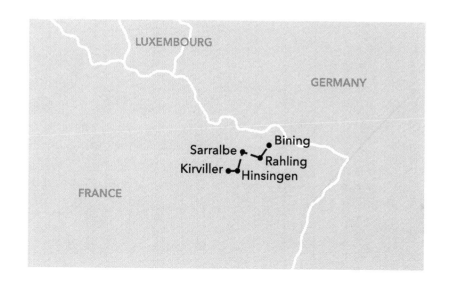

CHAPTER 6

Nursing a *Pferd*

WE FINALLY PULLED OUT of Givrycourt back to the same barn we had used in Torcheville around noon on Tuesday, November 28. Captain Kixmiller asked us to go back and look the field over, as he was not sure that all the casualties were out. We did so, and found three wounded men still alive. One died while we were there, but the other two made it; we evacuated them to the 3d Battalion aid station, which was still in Vittersbourg. We searched for Captain Willoughby's body, but failed to find it, although we did discover his map board. (We later found out from the civil-

35

ians in Honskirch that the German medics had evacuated an officer whose description fit Willoughby—and he was alive at the time.)

We stayed in Torcheville Tuesday night and Wednesday. We had hot showers, PX rations, and rest. Thursday found us setting up our aid station in Honskirch, the town that had caused us so much grief, and that the 2d Battalion had taken with little effort after we failed. We set up shop in the house where the Heinies had their CP when they were in town. The companies then moved northeast to Kirviller where we were busy guarding the division flank.

Colonel Menard[1] was relieved of battalion command while we were at Honskirch and Maj. William A. "Bucky" Callahan took over. The official reason they gave us was that Colonel Menard had been responsible for the fiasco of trying (and failing) to take the town, but I think all who know the facts will agree that the blame for that setback rests squarely on the shoulders of the higher-ups—regimental or division—who ordered the town to be taken with one battalion. It was too tough a nut for that number of men to crack as prior reconnaissance had shown; this was reinforced by subsequent investigation of the town's defenses. It had four complete double-apron barbed wire fences completely circling it, as well as a copious supply of mines, trenches, bunkers, etc.

Things were lively for us: while we were in a holding position, we were still sending out patrols and they got into plenty of trouble. On Thursday, Baker sent out a patrol north from Kirviller to investigate some bridges. It promptly got itself fired upon. The lieutenant in charge was killed and one man was wounded. He was left behind. Then came the usual hollering for medics to put on their red crosses and go get him. We respectfully requested a bit of covering artillery fire, as this was likely to be more effective than the Geneva Conventions, for it was a language the Krauts

---

1. Lt. Col. Noel Ambrose Menard. It should be noted that Colonel Menard received the Silver Star while serving as commander of the 1st Battalion, 328th Infantry.

appreciated. Capt. Bob Meade of Baker Company heartily agreed with us.

A few minutes later, we could see from Kirviller the shells bursting in the treetops near the machine gun that had started the trouble in the first place. Anyhow, Waryasz drove the jeep about a kilometer out of town until he came to a bridge that looked as if it were mined, while Meade and a couple of riflemen carried the wounded man from where he lay back to the jeep. We were not fired on.

The next day Baker moved into Hinsingen, just across the creek, and again a patrol was sent into the woods north of the town. The patrol was pinned down by small-arms fire and blasted with artillery. The aid station was still in Honskirch, but it so happened that we were in Hinsingen looking for a station site when the fireworks opened up, so we stuck around to make ourselves useful.

We could see all this happening from the Baker OP, which was in the top of a barn at the east end of town. We could also hear what was transpiring over the radio. By noon, those of the patrol who were unscathed as well as several walking wounded managed to get back under their own power. Larry Hrouda, the aidman with the patrol, was hit in the testicles; still, he not only patched up those whom he was unable to bring back, but also assisted another less seriously wounded man back with him.

Captain Meade called for artillery fire and the cannoneers promptly obliged as they had done the day before, this time firing about eight hundred rounds into the edge of the woods. This was an enormous number of shells, but it paid off in dividends, for the Heinies were too dazed to do anything about the litter squads that subsequently went out. To make doubly sure, Captain Meade took some riflemen into the little patch of woods to the east of town to cover the evacuation. This was accomplished without a shot being fired on either side. We evacuated the wounded to the regimental aid station in Altwiller, since we had to pass through that town to get to our own aid station in Honskirch.

Meanwhile, the boys were enjoying themselves in Honskirch. One of our aidmen, Raynes, who had been scheduled to go on the second Baker patrol, celebrated said assignment by going AWOL before the patrol.

Andy, Bruegge, and Menard took Lieutenant Mumme, the aforementioned S-2, up the local church steeple to frisk a dead German for information. There was a dud artillery shell in the steeple also, so Mumme didn't relish his job. Waryasz later took one of the Red Cross Doughnut Dollies, who was paying us a visit at Honskirch, on a private tour to see the same Heinie, for she claimed never to have seen one "in the flesh." Some date!

A local fellow came into the aid station to seek succor for his sick *pferd*. Andy was disgusted because just the day before, I had sent him to the wrong number (due to my faulty German translation) to look after a sick civilian, so he announced that he would have no more traffic with sick civilians' woes as interpreted by me. But when Bruegge overheard and became inquisitive, I told him that *pferd* was German for "daughter." So off he went, accompanied by the willing Watkins, their heads filled with visions of lovely German *frauleins* in distress. They returned slightly chagrined, having discovered that *pferd* actually translated to "horse." They did get a drink out of the deal, though.[2]

---

2. In his later notes, Marshall added: "They still don't know whether my translation was deliberate or faulty, and there's no point in ruining a good story by confessing at this late date."

CHAPTER 7

A Toe-Hold in the Fatherland

FROM HONSKIRCH WE MOVED for a couple of days' stay to Hinsingen, where things had settled down to a comparative quiet. I remember the surrender of a German cook who walked into our lines one night to give himself up. He said he had been cooking for four years and had been getting along fine, until somebody got the idea to make a rifleman out of him, which was more than he bargained for.

Tuesday, December 5, saw the battalion moving out to mount an attack in the woods to the north, where all the earlier trouble had occurred. A reconnaissance patrol had reported activity the night before, so we had an intense artillery preparation in which Dog Company's machine guns and mortars joined, as well as the .50-caliber and 37-mm antiaircraft tracked weapons.[1]

We watched the attack with field glasses from the loft of the barn, where we had established the aid station. Since the woods proved empty, it was a textbook operation, except for the four casualties that resulted from our own machine-gun fire and artil-

---

1. Marshall is most likely referring to the M15 (Combination Gun Motor Carriage) and its cousin, the M16 MGMC (Multiple Gun Motor Carriage). Both are M3 half-track variants: the M15 CGMC mounted an M1 37-mm gun and twin M2 .50-caliber machine guns, while the M16 MGMC featured the powerful M45 quad .50-caliber machine-gun turret. Originally conceived as an antiaircraft weapon system, the M16 MGMC was also adept at direct fire against ground targets in the infantry support role, for which it was nicknamed the "meat chopper."

lery. We saw them fall, called downstairs for the jeep to go after them, watched the aidman take care of them, then saw the jeep and litter squad arrive for the evacuation.

The troops pushed on through the woods heading for Sarralbe, still meeting no resistance. Beyond the four casualties from friendly fire, our only other one was Lieutenant Senger, whose jeep hit a mine on the east side of the same woods while he was trying to establish a supply route to the companies. He wasn't seriously injured, but the explosion left his face blackened with soot.

Before we had quite reached Sarralbe, the order came down to pull back into Hinsingen, which was accomplished just about dark. By midnight, the battalion had saddled up and we were off—to where we didn't know. All we knew was that we were heading east.

Wednesday morning's dawn found us sitting on the top of a hill on a muddy road midway between Schmittviller and Rahling. We were just in time to see a group of 4th Armored Division tanks lining up alongside us. They went barreling into the latter city after a short artillery preparation. They had used the road we stopped on for their line of departure. We felt that the whole German army could see us sitting there up on top of the world. It was the mission of the battalion, as we found out after much diligent searching and inquiring, to support the armor in their attack on Bining, the next town north of Rahling.[2]

As medics, we had to find a spot for the aid station quickly, as our own troops' attack was to get underway shortly. There was a farmhouse about halfway between the road we were on and Rahling (which the armor had passed by) so Denny Madden

---

2. The 1st Battalion of the 328th was attached to the 4th Armored Division from December 5 through December 8, 1944.

grabbed an M1[3] and set off to look the place over with Andy and me. I felt very self-confident with my trusty .45 as we proceeded to "capture" the farm. Its cellar was filled with civilians who gave us little trouble, although we later found out that two of them were deserters from the German army. The Heinies had been using the farm for an artillery position of some sort, but we found it ideal for the aid station.

We had no sooner gotten set up before business began—and we had customers aplenty! We were the only aid station anywhere in the neighborhood, so we got not only our own battalion casualties, but also those from the armor element. The armor seemed to be represented in the medical line solely by a tall, lanky redhead and a jeep. Every time we turned around, he was driving up in the jeep with a load of casualties, and then he'd be off for more. One time, this system was supplemented by a tank carrying wounded soldiers that drove right into the farmyard for direct evacuation into our aid station.

Late in the afternoon, an artillery aid station from the 4th Armored moved into the cellar. Since there were no artillery casualties, they were of little help. They refused to take any but their own—until we hollered at their colonel, after which the doctor-captain became more willing to pitch in and cooperate. Herbie Scheinberg had gone out as a temporary aidman with one of the companies and soon returned with a cut-up arm and had to be evacuated. He was one of our best men; fortunately, he was able to return to us at a later date.

The tanks were unable to get into Bining, so the task was turned over to the 1st Battalion and we got the job done. All did not go well and by dark there were a number of casualties in Bin-

---

3. Marshall is referring to the M1 carbine, which was smaller, lighter, and more practical for use by vehicle-borne troops than the M1 rifle (the "Garand")—the standard infantry long arm. Despite the similarity of nomenclature, the "United States Carbine, caliber .30, M1" was not just a foreshortened Garand, it was an entirely different weapon; the carbine employed a different operating mechanism and fired a different class of ammunition. The M1 carbine was produced in a number of variations, including a selective-fire version (M1A2) and a compact, folding-stock model designed for the use of paratroops (M1A1).

ing, so we set out to fetch them. The town was at least five kilometers from the farm and was burning merrily by the time we got there. We took one load out and instructed the company commanders to send the less seriously wounded back on the ration jeeps, then we sent out some men with a jeep to act as a collecting point.

In the wee hours of the next morning, the men and jeep returned with more casualties, while the battalion was relieved by the armor fellows. We didn't mind being relieved at all, but along with the notification of relief came an invitation to get the hell out of the farm and the area, and to get off the roads in a couple of hours. This really burned us up, but there was nothing we could do but comply, so off we went.

We swung back through Dehlingen and Oermingen back north to Etting where we joined the regiment again and settled down for the night. Major Parriot came to us as battalion exec to replace Captain Kixmiller who was kicked up to Division HQ. Father Bransfield arrived and said Mass for us in the field next to the aid station in the afternoon.

On Friday morning, December 8, we headed north to Wiedesheim, where we set up in a factory. After only a couple of hours, we lit out for Wittring. We stopped short of the town itself and established our station in the house of a Nazi sympathizer who had vamoosed, leaving plenty of evidence of his political sympathies. Apparently he had been an official in the local steel works.

The companies continued on toward Wiesviller, having no trouble to speak of that night, compared to events at the aid station. The coal stove in one of our rooms leaked; we found out just in time to save the six men sleeping there from asphyxiation. Andy had to give two of them artificial respiration. We had to evacuate one, Sam Solomon.

The next morning the troops got into Wiesviller and Woelfling,[4] so we backtracked around on the good road through

---

4. Wœlfling-lès-Sarreguemines

Achen[5] to follow them. Going down the hill into Wiesviller we got caught in an artillery barrage. Of all the things to do, the boys stopped the vehicles, piled out, and started running back up the hill. Finally, the barrage lifted. We lured the gang back and took off on the double. When we arrived in Wiesviller we took roll and found three of the men missing. I went back up the hill to scout for them. I found Geisler and headed back; Vella and Menard didn't make it back to the station until later that night.

We only paused for a few hours in Wiesviller, then moved over to the next town, Woelfling. Here we took over a civilian's house and set up for business. The lady occupant was not at all happy about the arrangement, complaining continually. There were apples galore in the house and a few odds and ends of chickens, so we ate fairly well. I taught Frank Valiga how to bake apples with sugar and cheese, so we had an epidemic of baked apples and cheese.

One time the boys were busy dissecting and cooking some chickens in the kitchen when the good lady decided to take inventory on her flock. She noticed the shortage and went searching. We hastily shut the kitchen door, posting a guard who informed her, when she came to that room to look, that the boys were taking a bath therein, so of course her presence would be intolerable. She went away and the chicken dinner proceeded.

I can't recall just what the troops were doing for the first couple of days of our stay in Woelfling, but I do remember the P-47s[6] gave the woods to the northeast of town a good going-over one afternoon. We watched the show from the attic of the house. On Tuesday the 12th, the troops got into the woods and the railroad station there and kept on moving. We were having little trouble ourselves, although the 2d Battalion (stationed on our right) was facing plenty of opposition.

---

5. This is the village of Achen, France—not to be confused with the German city of Aachen.

6. Built in greater numbers than any other U.S. fighter, the Republic P-47 Thunderbolt was a versatile fighter-bomber that could carry an ordnance payload approaching half that of the vaunted B-17 Flying Fortress. The P-47's hefty payload and outsize fuselage earned it the affectionate nickname of the "Jug."

That afternoon Denny Madden, Walt German, and I were out walking. We strolled over along the edge of the woods on our left flank, well behind our own lines. We found that the 35th Division on our immediate left had not moved, with the result that our own left flank was completely exposed for about a mile. The 35th had not gotten beyond the railroad that ran parallel to the front, whereas we were a good mile beyond it and still moving.

It was General Paul's fond desire to get some division elements into Germany proper, since the border was only about two miles from the railroad station in one spot. I would call this one of the most ignorant maneuvers of the war, exposing the flank for such a distance, merely to satisfy an old man's whim, but when the old man is also the commanding general, a whim often becomes an order. Fortunately, even the Heinies couldn't imagine anything so silly, thus Able Company managed to get a platoon across the border in the dark with little trouble.[7]

The 87th Division relieved us on the evening of December 12, and we were relieved in every sense of the word. They subsequently got the hell beat out of them and were forced to withdraw from the precarious position they inherited from us. It was a ticklish spot to get into, and we were all happy to leave it so promptly.

---

7. This occurred on the night of December 11, when a lone platoon from the 328th Infantry became the first element of the Yankee Division to set foot on German soil. With support from the 602d and 610th Tank Destroyer Battalions, the entire regiment pressed the attack across the German border in the morning, and by that afternoon had pushed six hundred meters into the Fatherland. When they were rotated off the front line that evening, the men of the 328th had concluded the Lorraine campaign.

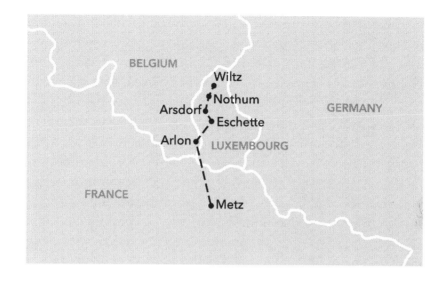

CHAPTER 8

The Bulge

WE PULLED BACK to a farm just north of Kalhausen and bedded down for the night. The following morning found us loading on trucks headed for a rest area in Metz,[1] where we happily settled into some barracks[2] in the city.

---

1. The regiment made the move to the citadel of Metz on December 13. At this point, the 328th had been engaged in active combat operations under the worst conditions possible for well over two months without a break.
2. The barracks in question was likely the Schlier Kaserne, a substantial three-story brick edifice which had served as quarters for students of the German Infantry Officers Candidate School prior to the city's capture on November 17.

City life proved enjoyable and we made the most of it. The regiment was quartered in what was apparently a military school of some sort, with real beds available for all, not to mention three hot meals a day, showers, movies, PX supplies—the whole nine yards! Passes were issued for those desiring to spend a day in the city proper. We did nothing in the line of training, merely policing our quarters and getting equipment and vehicles in shape.[3] I began to have more dermatitis around my ankles and lower legs, so I spent most of my time in the comfortable officers' quarters with my feet in a bucket of hot boric acid solution.

The window of our room looked out on the Moselle River about fifteen yards away. It was interesting to watch the little oar-propelled ferry boat doing a land-office business practically in our backyard. The Germans had thoughtfully blown all the bridges across the river in the vicinity, so the ferryman had plenty of customers.

We were very happy in Metz with everyone planning and hoping to spend Christmas there. Our hopes were shattered on Tuesday, December 19, when we were put on a twelve-hour alert. Several days earlier, Field Marshal Gerd von Runstedt had launched the Ardennes Offensive, which culminated in what would come to be known as the Battle of the Bulge. Patton's entire Third Army was being shifted north to cut into the Germans' southern flank.

Early Wednesday morning we were up and packed, although we didn't move out until almost noon. There was an air of mystery about the entire business. Nobody seemed to know where we were going or why. We were on our way, and that was that.

From Metz we moved north through Briey and Longwy and crossed into Belgium. When we reached the assembly area at Arlon we hooked east, heading across the border from Belgium

---

3. While the 1st Battalion medical detachment staff were relaxing, the 26th Division was in-processing and training fresh replacements—2,585 of them. These neophyte warriors would soon put their newly acquired skills to the test against the seasoned and increasingly desperate veterans of the Wehrmacht.

into Luxembourg. When we stopped for the night, we found lodging in a farmhouse right on the border slightly over a mile due east of the Belgian village of Guirsch. The aid station was now in Luxembourg with the battalion CP in Belgium, which made for a very cosmopolitan bivouac that night.

The civilian occupants of our combination farmhouse-barn were most perturbed about two major irritants at this time: the German advance and the moving of their threshing machine. The latter operation was performed by our medics, and almost resulted in disaster, for we moved it from solid cement flooring over onto what seemed to be the same, covered with hay, but which turned out to be lathing and plaster over the stall on the lower level. Fortunately, we did manage to wrestle it back before it fell through.

Barney Menard snagged a pass to Paris and made it back as far as regiment before division realized the enormity of the crisis we were facing and canceled all passes (their favorite reaction to any and all crises). I suppose the Metz interlude was still ringing in their ears when they authorized the pass in the first place.

The question on everyone's mind was: *Where were the Germans?* Nobody seemed to know.

We spent all day Thursday killing time around the farm. We could hear distant artillery, but it was far enough away so as not to be annoying. Not so for the civilians, for they finally packed all their belongings onto the family wagon, hitched the family stallions thereto, piled the family thereon, and blew.

Along toward evening we made ready to move and by dark were on our way. Capt. Harold Miller, the battalion S-1, had gone forward on a billeting detail, but he took the wrong road and hit a mine. He and his driver, a man named D'Amours, were both killed.

The battalion was to spend the night in a field on the hill directly south of Redange Attert, but we medics didn't relish the open-air accommodations. Instead, we decided to precede the troops on down into town. Major Parriot didn't like the idea, since we had yet to make contact with the Germans, but with a cry of "better captivity than pneumonia!" we swept into town, taking over the first house we came to. It was the first residence outfitted with electric lights that we'd seen since we left the States.

We bedded down, only to be aroused in a short while by 1st Sgt. Janakowski of Baker with a platoon of men whom Major Parriot had thoughtfully sent down to guard us. Chaplain McClung and his driver also put in an appearance before morning.

Early the next morning, we watched the line companies file by, heading north and followed by the 3d Battalion. We packed up and hit the road. At Ospern, the troops took off cross-country, so we headed for Hostert, hoping to intercept them. We were operating without a map of any sort, so at Hostert we made an executive decision and continued north toward Rambrouch, but it turned out to be a bum steer. Fortunately, some TD[4] men stopped us and warned us of enemy armor in that town, so we did an about-face and screwed but quick. We kept roaming around, finally finding the battalion about three kilometers east of Hostert, still heading north.

Tagging along through Eschette, we finally stopped in the woods three kilometers northwest of that village. We wanted to set up back in town, but Major Parriot nixed that idea. The companies started to dig in, when along came a German army sedan loaded with hot food. Evidently it was coming from Rambrouch headed for Eschdorf. The men tagged it, capturing the two soldiers inside. Pretty soon along came a motorcycle with a sidecar and two German medics whom the men also reeled in.

About this time, the brass began to suspect that the Germans might be hereabouts, so the men began to snoop around, and

---

4. TD is short for "tank destroyer," a class of armored vehicle, such as the M10 3-inch Gun Motor Carriage (Wolverine). The TD men in question possibly belonged to the 818th TD Battalion, which was attached to the 328th Infantry from December 21, 1944 to July 20, 1945.

surely enough, the patrols found some Heinies a couple of kilo-meters up the road around Heispelt. The Germans even had a light tank with them, which was most obnoxious. For over two hours I listened to the most asinine arguments and excuses between the TD officers and the tanker officer about whose job it was to settle the German tank. They argued and monkeyed around making reconnaissance until it became too dark—so they said—for either to move up.

Finally, Major Callahan and Captain Doyle became disgusted and sent a bazooka team from Able. They disabled the tank, set it on fire, and bumped off a couple of its fleeing occupants. This little action left the bazooka men okay, but a couple of covering riflemen were injured, so we went out to get them. We had no trouble ourselves, but it was most spectacular to creep by the burning tank in the darkness. The ammo inside was exploding, making it a proper inferno.

In the meantime, Andy Dedick had gone to Major Parriot, asking just what steps he should take to deal with the coming casualties, inasmuch as the major had been so adamant about not setting up the station in Eschette. The question put the good major in a flurry, so he digustedly told us to do as we saw fit. Back to Eschette went the aid station; Major Parriot bothered us no more about such decisions after that.

After setting up the station, we settled in for the night, while the doughs continued to dig in. Nobody seemed to realize that it was night. I had driven back up from Eschette to the companies to check their positions when along came Colonel Mott, the regi-mental exec, with the glad tidings that we had a ten-mile push ahead of us before morning.

Back to the aid station and we were soon packed up. The troops started forward while the battalion train headed north-west out of Eschette. We came to an abrupt halt almost as soon as the last elements cleared the village; up ahead, the Wehrmacht was contesting the advance of the rifle companies with grim determination. The fireworks centered around a sort of combination monument-water tower that was about three hundred meters west of the crossroads north of Wahl along the road leading to Rambrouch.

Our mission had been to locate the enemy and engage him. *Mission accomplished!*

CHAPTER 9

Christmas

THAT FRIDAY, DECEMBER 22, will be hard to forget. It was bitter cold with a brisk wind sweeping the road where we had stopped. The road ran along a ridge, and this exposed elevation just made it worse. The rifle companies kept calling for ammo and litters, but failed to send guides. Watkins and I started up once, but we heard Germans talking before we found the companies, so we beat it. Fred Warrick had the same experience.

This went on until about two the next morning when we finally contacted a guide who led us to the battalion CP at Redingshaff farm, about a kilometer south and slightly west of the contested monument-water tower. We found that everyone had settled in for the night, so we sent out squads to pick up what wounded we could find. It was practically daybreak before any of the casualties began to arrive at the farm. In the meantime, I was looking for a way to get a jeep down to the farm and having no luck. The guide had led us to a stream, which was unbridged and unfordable, while the only road we could see ran in front of the lines and to the farm. Using the road didn't seem like such a hot idea; rather, it was *too damn hot*, in spite of the chilliness of the night.

Finally, we had all the wounded assembled at the farm. The sun was up. We hand-carried the litter casualties to the vehicles on the road where the guide had met us. We let the walking wounded, the combat fatigued, and the frostbite cases work their own way along with us. The Germans could see the farm from Rambrouch, so they obligingly set up a machine gun and opened fire. Fortunately, the range was so great that they did no damage. In fact, at first we didn't even realize that they were firing at our little procession of litter teams and walking casualties.

When we reached the road—the same one where the battalion vehicles had spent the night, and down which we would have to go to get to the aid station, now in Eschette—we found the German machine gun doing its best to sweep the area. Jake came along and scoffed at such an incidental nuisance.[1] Madden suggested that the colonel take some walking wounded on his jeep into Eschette. He agreed, and Jake sailed off down the road with the Heinies dropping machine-gun slugs around his jeep as it tore along. Nobody was hit, but it was a good show. We still had two jeep-loads of wounded to go down that same road; we didn't much relish the idea of being sprayed with lead, even if the long range made hits pretty much a matter of chance.

Here I committed the greatest "tactical" error of my military career. Instead of taking some of the wounded riflemen who could walk to the edge of the woods and returning the fire, the gun being visible from that point, I elected to go back to Eschette, keeping below the ridgeline. There I knew I could get some supporting fire from the TDs or Dog Company to silence the enemy machine gun. I got back all right, but neither of the parties mentioned seemed the least bit inclined to help out—counting on them was my mistake. I was running around tearing my hair out when in came the two jeeps with Madden and Vella driving. They had gotten tired of waiting and decided to make a run for it. As in Jake's case they were fired on, once again without effect.

In the meantime, the Heinies varied the program by taking shots at the farm with a tank or a self-propelled artillery piece.

---

1. Jacobs was a no-nonsense commander; when word of the infamous Malmedy massacre of December 17 in which scores of American prisoners were gunned down in cold blood by their SS captors reached the 328th, his response was to issue an order on December 21 stating, "No SS troops or paratroopers will be taken prisoners but will be shot on sight." There is apparently no evidence that this no-quarter directive was carried out.

We began to wonder just where in hell the unit on our left was and why they didn't move into Rambrouch and save us all the wear and tear on our nerves. Such is war: often more happenstance than tactical brilliance.

Saturday afternoon Salvatore Glorioso and I put our heads together and figured that a trail we saw along the road might lead to the farm. We got in a jeep and tried it. Sure enough, we ended up at the farm, the first vehicle to get there. We took a couple more wounded back and set up a collecting point for the night in the farm. No casualties that night, though the companies were still unable to make any headway. I think we may have been waiting for the units on either side of us to catch up.

We were rather proud of our find—that is, the trail—for soon the infantry vehicles were wearing a set of ruts in it. By Sunday afternoon we had the aid station set up in the farmhouse with the action moving ahead. This time the battalion was headed for Arsdorf. Night came and found it poised on the hill overlooking that town. Andy Dedick had gone out and reported this situation on his return; I was soaking my feet in boric solution at the time. Meanwhile the order came from regiment to take the town, so our troops started in with a purpose. Since the Germans tried to hold, the call soon came for medics and we were on our way.

Christmas Eve is vivid in my memory. We crept over the snow glistening in the moonlight. Down a steep road leading into town from the east, we carefully made our way in both jeeps. A tank was blocking the road about halfway down the hill, so we had to wait until the driver moved it. Several burning houses supplemented the light of the moon, while the rumble of the tank's motor was occasionally accompanied by the crack of a rifle or a machine gun's harsh trill.

The CP was in the third or fourth house on the left-hand side of the road leading down into town. We stopped and went in. We were told that the companies had some casualties just up the

street; I recall Major Callahan saying that it would be a job getting them out inasmuch as bringing a jeep into town would be
impossible. He looked dumbfounded when I told him that we
medics had brought not one but two jeeps with us—and they
were in fact parked right outside. We didn't rest on our laurels
for long, but moved up to the companies' CPs. We soon had both
jeeps loaded with the more serious casualties and on their way
back for treatment.

In the meantime, Geisler and I, having called Captain Dedick
and told him to bring the station on in, went scouting about for
a likely spot. Our choice was limited because of the fighting
going on in the center of the village. We finally found a likely
house and entered. It was empty. We lit a candle and started a
fire. Just about then a Heinie burp gun[2] opened up outside. It
sounded as though the damn thing was right outside the front
window. Ed and I doused the light and whispered a few quick
prayers.

Then we decided that Andy should be told not to bring the
station to *this* house, but we wondered how to warn him—the
nearest field phone was in the battalion CP around the corner.
Neither of us felt like making the trip just then. Nevertheless, we
each loaded a carbine and ventured out to investigate. This we
did from the safety of our shaded doorway. We found that the
place was not in danger of immediate capture. As the burp gun
continued to fire, we realized that it was up on the hill—the
seeming nearness being attributable to the acoustics of the draw
in which our house stood.

We finally screwed up enough courage to go around to the
battalion CP where we met the aid station gang in the vehicles.

---

2. "Burp gun" is slang for any submachine gun (thanks to the common tactic of using short bursts
of automatic fire), but in this case Marshall is undoubtedly talking about the German MP40
submachine gun (often erroneously referred to as a "Schmeisser"). The *Maschinenpistole 40* was
extremely popular and extensively used by the German army. It was a relatively small weapon
that was much lighter and more manageable than its American counterpart, the Tommy gun,
thanks to its smaller-caliber cartridge (9-mm Parabellum), folding stock, and incorporation of
stamped-metal parts.

We repaired back to our house and opened for business, which was soon booming. Almost as many Germans and civilians were treated as GIs. The ambulance was still back at the top of the hill, so we evacuated to it ourselves by jeep.

That's how we passed our not-so-Silent Night.

Merry Christmas! Dawn found Arsdorf secure, with all the wounded taken care of. Sleep was quite in order, but our hard-earned slumber was disturbed by the news that we were to move out again. The general idea seemed to be that we were to force a crossing of the Sûre River north of Arsdorf.

Colonel Jacobs pulled what I would term one of the lowest tricks ascribable to humanity that afternoon. He knew that our men were exhausted and in no condition for anything, let alone a river crossing, so he told Major Callahan that the 3d Battalion (posted on our left) had already crossed the river and was therefore in fine shape to support our own crossing, which would be merely a troop movement rather than an allout fight.

Fortunately, Callahan took this news and the order with a grain of salt and did a bit of reconnoitering. It turned out that not only was the 3d Battalion *not* across the river, but it was not even up as far as we were on our flank. Jake had used a ruse to get us started across the river, but it backfired—the news leaked out and Jake was relieved of command.[3] We never did cross the

---

3. Colonel Jacobs was replaced by Lt. Col. Paul Hamilton (who had been serving on division staff) on December 26, 1944. For what it's worth, the Yankee Division had been given orders to force a crossing of the Sûre *without delay*, and III Corps command was putting serious pressure on General Paul to get his troops in gear and complete the mission. That pressure, of course, filtered down to the regimental commanders. Furthermore, prior to the 1st Battalion's attempt to cross the river, Colonel Jacobs had received a report that the 3d Battalion had seized the bridge in its sector at Bonnal and were in the process of securing the far bank. In fact, the bridge at Bonnal had been blown by the German rearguard (who were defending tenaciously) on Christmas morning. Jacobs hadn't tricked his men; it was just a classic case of the "fog of war."

Thea (Robert Marshall's daughter) notes:

Perhaps if Dad and my incredibly smart/thorough editor had been able to discuss this incident, my Dad would have changed his opinion. But, re-typing his work 50 years later, Dad still objected, as apparently many "boots on the ground" did at the time, to Colonel Jacobs' orders,

river, for while we sat outside of Arsdorf waiting, we were relieved by the 101st Regiment and we pulled back into the town.

Father Bransfield came around at suppertime and said our Christmas Mass for us in one of the houses. Several civilians were present and joined in the singing. It was a memorable service with at least one dead casualty in the room. I am at a loss for words to describe the celebration. Later in the evening we loaded up and pulled out for Buschrodt, where we went into the division reserve. We slept in a barn that night.

And that's what passed for "Christmas" for the medics of the 1st Battalion.

Early the next morning we moved into the village schoolroom. It was a light, airy place—ideal for an aid station. We settled down for a much-needed and well-appreciated rest. Our Christmas turkey dinner arrived on Tuesday. Better late than never.

The stay in Buschrodt was punctuated by a few odds and ends of interest. The dentists (Captain DeVito and Captain Golden) came and set up their chairs for business. The battalion officers threw a party that Dedick broke up by becoming plastered and telling the good Major McKillop just what he thought of him. The major was the regimental surgeon (which is to say, Dedick's boss), but the only time we ever saw him was while we were in a rest area.

The mail came in great quantity, especially packages, so there was plenty of choice chow. Our good friend Raynes, who had gone over the hill while we were in Honskirch, showed up claiming amnesia and an enjoyable stay in Paris whither his ailment had led him. He was promptly parked in the pokey to await court-martial. We left Buschrodt Saturday morning, December 30, our departure punctuated by a plume of smoke billowing from under Joe Vella's jeep. After extinguishing the flames, we

---

believing them to be trickery. So, trickery, bad intelligence, "fog of war," downward pressure, whatever—this daughter is grateful that Major Callahan undertook that extra reconnaissance!

Capt. Tony DeVito, Bayreuth, Germany, 1945. Photo courtesy of Ann Hall Marshall.

did some investigating and discovered he had left the emergency brake on and it caught fire. We were soon under way again, our destination the village of Bavigne.

Creeping along in convoy as we were, it took all morning to reach the place. The morning ride was very chilly. We set up our aid station in a couple of rooms in the same building being used by the 101st. The battalion mission was merely to hold the town and fill the gap between the 101st and the troops on our left. We didn't expect much business, but we were hardly settled in before Able's kitchen truck was hit on its way into town. One of the several casualties died. Major Callahan went back with a fever and Major Parriot assumed command of the battalion.

The town was subject to an occasional shell of the 120-mm mortar type. They delivered a terrific concussion; one of the artillerymen was killed outright by the intense shock waves. The impacts were very demoralizing as well, but with some good effects—the regiment had moved into the village in all its glory, proceeding to take over all the half-decent buildings. The 1st Battalion had very slim pickings by way of accommodations. The regimental HQ had moved in with great fanfare, but shortly after the arrival of several of the 120-mm shells, they went streaming out of town to the rear.

After that we had a little peace of mind with some room to move around in. I spent my evenings in the loft of the barn that was connected to the building that housed the station; it was most comfortable. On the other hand, the "Gopher Boys" moved into the cellar, staying there when they weren't out for chow. It was a small, undesirable place, but they appreciated the overhead cover.

Able company picked up several Heinie patrols as they tried to get into town (for what, I don't know). We didn't mind Able's killing or capturing the patrols, but when they took to wounding them then hollering for us medics, we began to balk. Their inaccurate shooting was putting us to a lot of unnecessary work.

CHAPTER 10

Screaming Mimis

WE NEXT HEADED FOR Kaundorf, where we set up in a house, while the troops were in an assembly area north of town. As far as our own men were concerned, there was no trouble that first night, but the 3d Battalion was having a rough time around Schuman's farm at the crossroads north of Nothum. Since their aid station was also in Kaundorf, we pitched in and helped with their casualties.

We went out that night to contact our companies and had our introduction to the "Screaming Mimis," a rocket projectile fired in groups of six.[1] Most of the GIs hated them, but we found them to be not too bad, since one could hear the discharge, and thus have time to duck and cover before they landed. In spite of such an "attractive" feature, we decided the companies didn't need contacting that particular night.

The following day we set up a collecting point in a couple of barns just south of Nothum on the way to Mecher-Dunkrodt. The line companies were to move that night through Nothum into the woods north around Schuman's farm. At first we weren't going to move the station, but no sooner had we settled in for the night than we got a call, so we decided to move into Nothum. At first we

---

1. "Screamin' Mimi" (aka Moanin' Minnie") refers to a family of German rockets collectively called *Nebelwerfer* (smoke mortar, a misleading moniker intended to evade prewar armaments restrictions). The nickname was coined to describe the unnerving high-pitched noise the rockets made in flight. Marshall likely encountered the Nebelwerfer 42 (NbW 42) variant that fired six rockets in a ripple salvo.

A "screaming mimi" rocket projector. Photo, public domain, provided courtesy of Aden Nichols.

only took part of the station up. It was here that I performed my first and only "surgical procedure" while in the ETO. It was questionable at best. We were trying to get a plasma needle into a GI with a belly wound, but his veins were collapsed. So, remembering all my Barkeley[2] baloney, I decided on a venesection. I cut transversely over the unfortunate chap's wrist where I thought there was a faint pulse, not knowing whether veins or arteries made for a pulse. I was getting nowhere, when the poor fellow woke enough to see what was going on. He began to thrash about enough to raise his blood pressure and to fill his veins enough for Nick to get a needle in. We gave him three units of plasma, but he died of internal bleeding in the ambulance after leaving the aid station in Kaundorf. I had ridden back to the station with this casualty on the jeep. Andy returned with me to Nothum for the night. The balance of the station followed in the morning.

2. Camp Barkeley was a major training installation near Abilene, Texas. In addition to hosting infantry and armor troops, Camp Barkeley was the home of the Medical Administrative Corps Officer Candidate School.

+ + +

By Sunday morning, January 7, our most hectic week in the ETO was under way. The tactical situation deserves mention: We were trying to get into Wiltz from the southwest (from the town of Nothum), but the terrain and the German army had other ideas. I believe the 3d Battalion was on our immediate right, while one of the other two regiments was beyond them. I don't know who was on our left. After a day or two, the 90th Division passed through us and took up that position.

The Germans had artillery and rocket launchers all around Wiltz, with no apparent lack of ammo for same. They also used tanks and self-propelled guns to break the monotony. The ground around Wiltz was higher than that around Nothum, so the Krauts were looking down our throats the whole time.

We located in the lower part of town, so we were not under direct observation, but not low enough to escape the artillery fire. To get to the companies, we had to run the road to Schuman's farm. This put us very much in the open and exposed. For the first couple of days we were taking fire from three sides, but then some American elements got into Berlé (to the northwest), eliminating some trouble from that direction, while the troops on our right moved up, and the line was straightened out.

The battalion CP was in a house at the eastern (and highest) end of the village. Just what jackass picked this choice location I don't know, but it was a dilly. The Heinies could see the place perfectly from the Wiltz area and they let go every time they saw something move. A tanker colonel got killed right outside the CP, while our own regimental CO, Colonel Hamilton, was stuck there for several days because of the intense fire.

We experienced a thorough bombing and strafing job one day. There were reports that our own planes were responsible, but I never could find anybody who stayed outside long enough to identify them. Our ack-ack opened up on them, but they didn't hit a thing—likely, they were firing by remote control from the cover of the cellars.

For the first day or two we were the only aid station in town. We did a land-office business, so much so that we finally had to complain to Colonel Hamilton. We were handling casualties from all three of the 328th Regiment's battalions as well as some from the 90th Division—and everybody was having plenty of casualties. I don't know the exact figure, but in one twenty-four-hour stretch we topped the two hundred mark—I believe that was January 9.

At first we had our collecting point in Schuman's farm. Jackson Kahner, a lieutenant and one of our perennial headaches, got himself scratched and evacuated again. Harry Doyle, by this time a captain and CO of Able Company, got the full effects of a blast and was sent back for good. Two of our aidmen, Gray and Kliver, went back with wounds. Kraft was another aidman who got knocked out of the picture. Captain Kuligowski—the very same chap who had gotten lost at Berange farm—got himself lost again and captured. Sergeant Gonta from the anti-tank platoon was hit while he was fixing a truck for us to take out. Eddie Geisler and Morgan Madden were wounded at the same time. Coke went back with a bad case of nerves and Lt. Clark Reynolds of Baker was hit. Dancy got it in the hand.

Enough of human casualties! Our vehicles likewise suffered. A small mortar shell dropped squarely on the hood of one of our jeeps that was parked out in the woods waiting for business. Another shell burst outside a window of the station; we got only the concussive part of the blast inside, but a Dog Company man on guard across the street was killed, the jeep was put out of running order, and Dedick's and my bedrolls (which were in the back of the vehicle) were filled with shrapnel. Our other jeep stashed out in the woods got a couple of flat tires from flying shrapnel.

The run between Nothum and Schuman's farm was exposed and hot. Jenkins, Madden, Waryasz, and Vella—the jeep drivers—opened the engines up wide until it seemed like they were about to become airborne. The trouble with this system was stopping in the snow. At one point, the battalion actually got on the hills overlooking Wiltz, but was forced to withdraw because supply and evacuation were impossible through the woods and then across open country.

The anti-tank and A & P gang pitched in and helped us all the time, in manning the collecting points and acting as litter bearers. Even Tony Geydos was pried out of the CP to pinch-hit as MAC officer in charge of night evacuation one evening when I felt the "eighty-eight shakes"[3] creeping up on me. I decided to ease off that night, and Geydos was unhappy with the assignment. However, he subsequently confessed that he felt he did more for the war effort that night than any other he spent in the ETO.

The booby prize for the week went to the 2d Battalion lieutenant who got on the radio and announced *in the clear* to his correspondent that the Heinies had his particular spot zeroed in with their mortars. Until then only an occasional shell dropped in, but the Jerries must have been listening, for they stopped their searching fire to concentrate on that particular spot. Our personal objection to this turn of events was that the 1st Battalion forward CP and one of our collecting points were less than twenty-five yards distant.

Father Bransfield said Mass in the kitchen of the house across the street and was literally almost blasted out of the pulpit by an incoming shell. Another time Bruegge had just left the outside corner of one of our own rooms when a shell burst sheared off said corner. All in all, the aid station was hit about five times, though no fragments actually got into the rooms to cause damage. Andy performed one of his rare amputations, while Joe Senger snagged *another* Purple Heart.

Editor's note: Displaying that remarkable humility that distinguished so many of these ordinary men who performed extraor-

---

3. GI slang for shell-shock or combat fatigue (and a reference to the ubiquitous—and dreaded—German artillery piece, the eighty-eight).

dinary feats, Marshall failed to note that he was awarded the Silver Star (only two steps down from the Medal of Honor) for his actions during this desperate winter engagement between Nothum and Wiltz. The text of his award citation fills in the details:

> For gallantry in action near Nothum, Luxembourg, on 9 January 1945. During the attack on the enemy forces in the vicinity of Nothum on 9 January 1945, First Lieutenant Marshall, First Battalion medical administration officer, organized and assisted the operations of litter squads as they moved forward with the attacking companies. During the course of the operations, three vehicles which were being used to evacuate the casualties were struck by enemy mortal shells. With utter disregard for personal safety, while under continuous enemy fire, First Lieutenant Marshall rushed forward and, moving from vehicle to vehicle, extricated those too badly hurt to help themselves. He then carried the wounded to the side of the road where he immediately administered to them. As he worked, he directed other aid men treating the less seriously wounded and was instrumental in maintaining an orderly and efficient removal of the casualties while enemy shells continued to harrass [sic] all activity in the immediate area. He worked steadily and, although physically exhausted, remained with the casualties until all had been evacuated. His heroic actions and inspiring leadership were directly responsible for the saving of numerous lives and preserving the morale of the troops. His solicitude for our wounded, his outstanding courage and his unusual devotion to duty reflect the highest credit upon First Lieutenant Marshall and the armed forces of the United States.

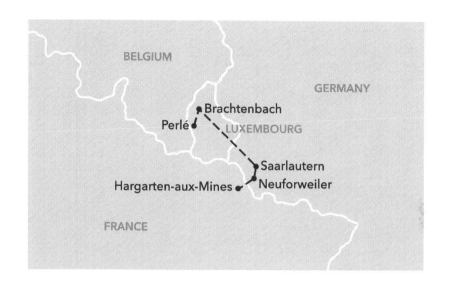

CHAPTER 11

Court-Martial

ON JANUARY 13 the troops were scheduled to take over a holding position northeast of Berlé, so we went up in the morning to pick out a location for the station. The village was in sorry shape—as bad as any we had seen so far—but we did find a barn with one fair-sized room still in decent shape. Some of the medics stayed there, while the rest of us moved up that night. We had to go around by way of Bavigne, and we had quite a ride.

The moon was up, but snow had covered the vehicle tracks across the fields, so we were traveling cross-country for the last kilometer or so. We arrived to find that the men already had two

The Aid Station referred to in the text, presumably in Berlé,
Luxembourg, January 1945. Photo courtesy of Ann Hall Marshall.

customers from the 90th Division. They had been wounded and
knocked unconscious the day before. Their frostbite was almost
worse than their wounds. We kept them in the station for the
night, evacuating them the next day. Father Bransfield said Mass
in the station on Sunday.

Captain Golden relieved Andy and me while we went back to
Longwy to testify in Raynes' court-martial. On our way back from
this two-day trip, we stopped at Perlé where Andy's fiancée, Kate
Golden (no relation to the captain), was nursing with the 16th Field
Hospital. The indoor heat and too much festive champagne got to
Andy, so we cut our visit short and proceeded to Longwy.

Lt. Kate Golden, with the 16th Field Hospital, who later married Capt. Andy Dedick. Photo courtesy of the Dedick famiy.

The champagne effects lasted into the officers' mess that night. Dedick decided he didn't like one Major O'Brien's looks, so he started to tee-off on him. A Captain Budd and I forcibly restrained our good doctor who had gotten O'Brien by the lapels and was winding up. We apologized for Andy to the offended major by explaining that this was really combat fatigue, not intoxication. Imagine our surprise at the court-martial the next day to find that Major O'Brien was president of the court! He asked some very pointed questions about combat fatigue in connection with Raynes' case, but which we knew were not concerned particularly with Raynes. Captain Kixmiller was on the court; he sat there grinning all throughout the proceedings.

That night, Friday, January 19, we were back in Perlé at the 16th Field Hospital. Only one room was available, so I undressed and hit the sack, reveling in the clean sheets, while Andy and Kate parked on a cot across the room. I guess they were whispering sweet nothings to each other, but I was out cold. I suspect they didn't appreciate my unconscious chaperoning. It was the first

Captain Dedick, Lieutenant Golden, and Lieutenant Marshall in Perlé, Belgium, January 1945. Photo courtesy of Ann Hall Marshall.

time they'd been "alone" together since they left the States, so I doubt they paid much attention to yours truly.

We had a cold Saturday drive back to Berlé, arriving to find we were to move out the next morning. So we continued on, stopping in Doncols for the night. The idea seemed to be that we were to force the Wiltz River north of Doncols Sunday morning. Major Parriot took most of the officers forward to reconnoiter the crossing area that night. We decided to move the aid station into the railroad station. Plans were very well laid out; before dawn we moved out of Doncols, silently as Indians, into the railroad station and set up. With the coming dawn, the artillery and mortars opened up. Dog Company machine guns fired tracers over our heads. We could see bursts in Grumelschied to the southeast.

What few Germans were in the neighborhood surrendered quickly, so the troops continued with little opposition. We had no casualties. Father Bransfield came up and celebrated Mass. Chaplain Gordon put in an appearance and immediately started egging us to get rid of the German corpses that were around the station, having been left there by the 90th when we relieved them. It was times like these that made us miss our buddy, Chaplain McClung, who had been evacuated from either Kaundorf or Nothum. He never chivvied us over such trivialities.

Andy and I spent the evening driving around trying to find the companies, but finally gave it up for a bad job. Eventually we discovered that they had gotten into Brachtenbach, so we sent out a collecting point and settled down for the night.

The next morning, we packed up and left the railroad station and took our whole dog and pony show to Brachtenbach. There we set up in a house that the Germans apparently had been using for medical purposes. They had a full graveyard across the street; they had been "burying" their dead by laying the corpses on the ground and then heaping some dirt on them. In fact, they had left so hurriedly that there were still several bodies in their makeshift morgue, a shed in the front yard.

From Brachtenbach, Andy and Captain Golden (who had stayed with us) went back to the clearing company. Their purpose was to get Lieutenant Sauders removed from his job as communications officer and out of the battalion. He had become afraid of his own shadow.[1]

In the meantime, we started to move Tuesday night, January 23, north and east to the village of Eselborn, then occupied by a cavalry group. Wednesday found us set up in a carpentry shop at the top of a hill, on a road leading down into the railroad station at Clervaux. This time the troops were to force a crossing of the Clerve River and head east to the German border. As it developed, crossing the Clerve was a lot tougher than crossing the Wiltz.

---

1. Sauders might have been suffering from combat fatigue, or what is now recognized as post-traumatic stress disorder (PTSD).

Streepey had come to take Andy's place while he was back at Boulaide at the clearing company. The Heinies threw three shells in the vicinity of the aid station; down into the cellar went Streepey, burrowing into a corner. He scarcely stopped to say hello to Andy who returned Wednesday morning, but took off like a broad-assed bird for the rear immediately upon Andy's arrival.[2]

Along toward this time the fireworks really began. The troops were stopped on the high ground overlooking the river, the valley, and the town by the Germans who occupied similar positions on the opposite hillside. The 3d Battalion was on our right, the boundary being the draw and the road that ran down it past our station. At the bottom of the draw was a barn that we had decided to use as a collecting point. This caused us no end of trouble; Al Bowman, who was at the head of Baker, seemed unable to locate it. Bowman was another Kuligowski—never knew what the score was. He had his casualties everywhere except in the barn when we went looking for them.

In the afternoon we went down to the barn to check the route. We picked up an assortment of wounded from both our own and the 3d Battalion. The latter's medical jeep had been fired on by a machine gun (or guns), shooting from the opposite hill, so they had rounded up a scout car[3] from somewhere and persuaded it to go down to the barn with them. The scout car was using its .50-caliber machine gun[4] to snipe at the other hillside, so the Germans laid low. We decided to make our little tour while the car was still there.

I walked down to the bottom and, having encountered no trouble, signaled to Denny to bring the jeep, which he did. We passed Major Mattingly on the way down and stopped to ask him

---

2. Possibly, Streepey was suffering from a malady similar to that of Lieutenant Sauders.

3. The M3/M3A1 Scout Car was a wheeled armored vehicle that could transport an infantry squad of seven men and provide fire support with three machine guns (one .50 caliber and two .30 caliber) mounted on a skate rail around the hull. The Scout Car was also used as an ambulance.

4. This is the legendary Browning M2 HB (heavy barrel) .50-caliber machine gun, known affectionately as "Ma Deuce." It can be effectively employed by ground troops (mounted on a tripod) or by armored vehicles against infantry, lightly armored vehicles, and even slow, low-flying aircraft. A real war-horse, it is still in the army inventory.

where his 3d Battalion troops were. Then the scout car pulled out, we loaded up, and screwed. As we were going back up the road, we passed Mattingly walking down.

Back at our station we unloaded and were taking care of the patients when another jeep arrived and unloaded, since we were the first aid station along the road. The one guy was in sad shape, but Andy got plasma into him. It didn't do much good—he died right there. His face was ashen gray. Not until I heard Barney checking the dog tag did I realize that the face belonged to Mattingly. About the same time, Floyd Laudenslager was also fatally wounded, dying in our station. He had been demoted from assistant to Captain Golden to an aidman—regimental politics. Lieutenant Barnes of Charlie was also wounded and later died, either on the way to, or in, the hospital.

The night of January 24, 1945, was a busy one. I didn't go out myself, but the men were on the go all the time, first chasing around buildings at the bottom of the hill looking for casualties that Bowman kept hollering about, then working over the hill itself to bring in the wounded from there.

The next morning the battalion crossed the river and took off after the Heinies. We had been able to see them pulling out the night before from the second floor windows of the carpentry shop where we'd set up.[5] The troops didn't have a whole lot of trouble. Charlie Company was returning machine-gun fire with interest, and with interesting results.

We decided to move down to some houses at the foot of the hill. While we were picking out a likely house, some blasted Heinie mortar began firing from a position to the south and east. Its shells were landing right around the houses. Our advance party had quite a time ducking from house to house.

Behind one hotel we found a cave into which the Germans had crowded area civilians when they had come through six weeks

---

5. Von Runstedt's desperate Ardennes offensive came to a close on January 25. The Yankee Division had played a crucial role in driving the Germans back and relieving the besieged troopers of the 101st Airborne, the "Battered Bastards of Bastogne."

earlier. There were between one and two hundred of these unfortunates. They had not been allowed to leave the cave during these six weeks, so they were especially happy to see us Americans. The 28th Division had been holding this area when von Runstedt's offensive overran it. They had taught the civilians a few GI expressions; it was amusing to see a woman duck a landing shell, then look up and say, "Oh, my achin' back!" or "Strictly on the beam!"

No sooner had we set up in the hotel mentioned—a lovely room—when a call came from battalion about casualties in Urspelt, whither the companies had gone. We had been waiting for the engineers to get a bridge across the river, but the mortar shelling caused delays. Apparently there was artillery as well. The Heinies must have run out of ammo, as around noon they surrendered—but still no bridge seemed likely in the immediate future, though the engineers had been loitering about all morning.

Cacchia, Cohen, Daigle, and I loaded some equipment on our backs and started on foot for Chateau d'Urspelt. No sooner had we arrived at the first buildings than the Germans threw a few artillery shells at the place, in what seemed to us at the time an over-personalized welcome.

In spite of the urgency of the calls, the couple of casualties we treated weren't seriously hurt, so we tended to them as well as some German wounded. The battalion CP was in the cellar of the chateau itself, so we set up in the first-floor kitchen. About nine o'clock Andy and the jeep arrived, the bridge having finally been completed, so we sent the wounded back. The rest of the men stayed back in the hotel for the night, then moved up at daybreak on Friday, January 26.

CHAPTER 12

Living in a Tavern

THE DOUGHS PUSHED ON to Fischbach, stopping there. Able CP had been in the chateau living room, so when they moved out, we moved in. We spent the night around a roaring fire in the only fireplace we'd seen so far in our European travels. HQ Company kitchen staff picked up a PW for KP and was enjoying the novelty of the arrangement.[1] Andy and Morgan went to Fischbach for a couple of GI and Heinie wounded and started them back.

Saturday we were relieved by a unit of the 35th Division, so we pulled back to an assembly area around Brachtenbach. After resting for a couple of hours, we pulled out around midnight heading south. We rode all night and it was colder than hell. Passing through Bavigne, Arsdorf, Arlon, Luxembourg City, after the usual mix-ups and wrong turns, with Geydos leading the column, we detrucked at Dalem, a French village halfway between Boulay-Moselle and Saarlautern (Germany).[2] This was Sunday morning.

Late that afternoon I headed for the Saarlautern area with some other officers. We were to relieve a battalion of the 95th Division, which was holding the towns of Lisdorf and Wadgassen, south of Saarlautern. Our station was set up in Neuforweiler to be equidistant from these towns. The battalion CP was in Holzmühle.

---

1. Of course "PW" is a prisoner of war and "KP" is that bane of all servicemen, kitchen patrol—which should be relegated to a PW whenever possible.
2. Renamed Saarlouis in 1945.

The 95th medics were very cordial, hosting me to an elegant supper right there in their station, which was in the village pastor's rectory. They explained their evacuation routes, adding that things had been so quiet for the past month that they had never used them. By dark I was back in Dalem to spend the night.

We were to move the station up to make the exchange the next afternoon. Jenkins, Madden, and I spent the next morning on a hill above Dalem trying our luck shooting the elusive mark with a P38 and a 9-mm Belgian automatic.[3] The session was not successful, so we decided that there must be something wrong with the pistols!

The night before the boys had celebrated with some local alcohol that turned out to be potent, judging from its effects. Madden busted up a perfectly good blackjack game by insisting upon playing while under the influence.

Our exchange was made without incident. It wasn't complete until midnight, so the 95th medics hung around until then. They seemed very reluctant to leave such an elegant setup, while we were congratulating ourselves on having been lucky enough to rate such a deal after our rough and cold session up in Luxembourg.

Our new position really amounted to a rest area under combat conditions. All the troops were in warm houses with beds to sleep in. The civilian residents had all been evacuated either by the Germans or our own forces; indeed, except for the kitchens and the A & P platoon, we had the entire village to ourselves. Occasionally a battery of self-propelled 155-mm rifles[4] would move into the field back of the rectory; windows tended to get broken by the concus-

3. Marshall is referring to the Walther P38 9-mm semiautomatic pistol, which replaced the P08 Luger as the standard sidearm of the German army, and to the Browning Hi Power 9-mm semiautomatic pistol. Though based on a design by an American, John Browning, the Hi Power was produced by Fabrique Nationale (FN) in Herstal, Belgium. Enormously popular, due in part to its thirteen-round magazine capacity, the Browning Hi Power has been used by fifty armies worldwide (to include those of both the Allied and Axis powers in WWII).
4. The 155-mm Gun Motor Carriage (GMC) M40 had only been introduced in the ETO in March, 1945. It was essentially a 155-mm M1 Long Tom rifle mounted on a modified M4A3 Sherman tank chassis.

sion of their firing. On the other hand, I don't think a single enemy shell landed in town while we were there.

Across the street was a large garage that proved to be an excellent pistol range. With the door shut, no sound of firing could be heard for any distance. We brushed up on our shooting with GI .45s as well as a Heinie 9-mm Schmeisser machine pistol that some Able GIs had gotten for me up in Ravigne. Joe Vella tried out his P38, but like Andy, he tended to bank his bullets into the bull's-eye off the concrete floor. This was somewhat dangerous, so Joe was convinced to desist and turn his attention instead to cooking up a batch of spaghetti; he insisted on calling it macaroni, but by either name it was a real treat. George Trabucco and I also tried *our* hands at creating something that resembled spaghetti. It was gratefully consumed, but I cannot vouch for its quality. Geisler tried his hand at apple turnovers with fairly decent results.

While a resident of Neuforweiler, I was fashioned into a second-class poker player. I was caught in the hideous coils of this game of chance, and there was no escape. Bruegge, Andy, Nicolo, Jenkins, Vella, Waryasz, and others all took turns taking my dough. They did a thorough, professional job, leaving me a win every so often so that I would not get disgusted and quit. Andy taught us a version called "baseball"—seven-card stud with practically all the cards in the deck being wild. It looked easy to me. The pots were large, but every time I got "up to bat" I struck out.

Much earlier shelling had scattered hundreds of books around the front rooms of the house and out into the yard. I managed to salvage several Latin books that I shipped home. I still have the German-Latin missal I liberated. I had better luck holding on to it than I did with the Bible that I lifted from the rectory in Lohr.

Father Bransfield said Mass in Holzmühle, so we piled in the jeep and attended that Sunday. From the brewery in Saarlautern and from one in Metz came a couple of barrels of beer. While the beer experts pronounced the Metz brew superior, both barrels were consumed with alacrity and zest. Andy also got a treat: a large box of medical instruments that one of the GIs had picked up for him in Wadgassen.

Our total casualties for the week were two: Sergeant Tucker from the A & P platoon set off a booby trap in the woods near Wadgassen, sustaining only scratches; and on the day we were being relieved by one of the other regiments, one of their advance party monkeyed with another booby trap—one of our own—in Wadgassen and got belted. The new medics were just in the process of moving in, so Andy hopped in the jeep, drove down, patched him up, and brought him back to the aid station.

We loaded the casualty into the ambulance, climbed into our own vehicles, and set off for Hargarten-aux-Mines back in France. I had gone there that morning to make arrangements for taking possession of the aid station from the outfit that had been there previously. In Hargarten lived Mama and Papa, who had a saloon instead of children. More fastidious types might call it a taproom. Into this tavern came our aid station for a more pleasant week even than the one in Neuforweiler. Mama baked all sorts of German pastries for us when we supplied the ingredients. She also washed our clothes. Papa tended the fire and manned the bar. What an ideal arrangement! We procured more beer from Metz, thus putting Papa's coils[5] and bar to the use for which they were created.

Andy and Barney Menard set off for Paris the day after we arrived. Streepey waddled in with his cot and a bedroll that needed a jeep trailer for transportation. There was little excitement in Hargarten. The regiment had moved into Falck, the adjacent town, and showed movies nightly in the theater in that place. The Doughnut Girls honored us with a visit. The men were sleeping in upstairs rooms across the street. Apparently they found some entertainment there in fraternizing with their civilian hosts and hostesses.

I vividly remember the night I was taking a bath in the barroom that had running water. I was attired as most people are when bathing and was busily at work removing the strong odor

---

5. Marshall is referring to the coils of metal tubing used in taverns and pubs to cool down continuous-draw, room-temperature beer.

of he-goat from my hide when in walked Mama. She was looking for *bilderbuches*[6] (that is, *Life* magazines) and wasn't the least embarrassed, so I caught the spirit of the occasion and helped her find them. She thanked me and left. I both blushed and laughed, for I had not even the modesty of a towel.

Around February 15, we left Hargarten for Saarlautern proper. The fighting was getting closer this time, though the 104th Regiment, which we were relieving, reported only occasional casualties. Our aid station was in a ground-level air raid shelter on the east bank of the Saar River, just across the bridge. The troops and the battalion CP were farther north in the Saarlautern suburb of Roden.

When we relieved the 104th, we had to place tiny crosses of luminous tape on the vehicle bumpers before being allowed to cross the bridge. Also, word was out that anybody wearing a long overcoat, or not carrying a gas mask, was to be shot on sight.[7] All were very fastidious about guards and countersigns. Apparently the 95th Division had enlivened their long weeks in these positions sending out information and sabotage patrols, with full reciprocation by the Germans. The cautious 26th was taking no chances.

I think "cautious" may be the wrong word here. The 95th had suffered practically no casualties, but no sooner had we settled into our air raid shelter than business started popping. First of all, some of the brass decided we should complete the capture of Saarlautern and its suburbs. The situation we inherited was pretty much 50-50—the town proper on the west bank was completely ours, but the suburbs on the east bank were held partly by GIs and partly by Heinies. The Siegfried Line ran along the east bank and was very wide here. We had taken some of its pillboxes, but the majority were still in enemy hands. The buildings of the town

---

6. Literally, "picture books."

7. The American gas mask carrier was a canvas pouch, whereas the Germans carried their gas masks in distinctive fluted metal cylinders. As the Americans and the Germans were both wearing long overcoats during the winter, the gas mask carrier was a handy visual aid to identify friend or foe.

were pretty well leveled. This leveling process continued all the time we were there.

The 95th Division and our 104th Regiment had been content to leave well enough alone after they had taken as much of the town as they turned over to us, but the 328th decided to begin knocking its head against the stone wall in more ways than one. It was so futile to try to advance, for every captured pillbox had two more behind ready to give twice as much trouble.

The line was very deep in these parts, extending back into Germany for some miles. The house-to-house fighting was of the worst sort, for the Germans had ample time to booby-trap all the houses in our line of advance. They also benefitted from the supporting fire of the pillboxes that were indestructible from any but the closest range.

We had our hands full. Major Parriot wanted a collecting point in the battalion CP. Between there and the aid station, the road ran across open ground with a bridge over a swampy section. This was a short half-mile, but it seemed interminable to anyone passing over it, thanks to an uncaptured pillbox that swept the road with machine-gun fire whenever there was traffic. The bullets caused no casualties, but vehicle accidents due to jeeps racing up or down the road to avoid the bullets were not uncommon. One bad wreck: two jeeps traveling at dusk in opposite directions, each going like a bat out of hell, met head on. There were a few broken limbs from that one!

Our casualty rate was steady. Almost every day we could expect a dozen or so wounded to drift in or to get carried in by the men manning the collecting point. Every so often a company would be ordered to take the next row of houses, and then would come a call for the medics.

In between such little forays, German booby traps, artillery, and mortars produced more customers for us. The odd part of it all was that after fighting like hell for a couple of houses and taking them, we would either be pushed back or forced to withdraw because the crossfire would break up communication. Joe Armstrong, 1st sergeant of our HQ company, was killed by a shell when he stepped outside the CP to use the latrine.

And then there was this: While the 95th reported that the Germans were honoring the red cross of the Geneva Conventions, our experience was contrary.

All was not work at the aid station. Evenings it was poker, days we rummaged around town. A drug store that had been pretty well looted and torn up nonetheless yielded boric acid powder and suppositories—both much needed. A seven-gallon pump-type fire extinguisher with a long hose became a serviceable ersatz shower; we could heat it full of water on the stove, then turn it over to a man to pump and a man to shower. Tony DeVito, our regimental dentist (along with Golden) furnished a shower-head for the end of the hose.

The kitchens were set up in the city proper in a barracks, so we sent the jeep back at mealtimes to pick up hot chow. Lieutenant Williams had stored his ammo somewhere near the kitchens. The Heinies dropped a shell into his dump one evening, blowing the stuff sky-high. Nobody was injured, but Willie had a red face for a while after that.

One night an ambulance driver brought Andy a note from Kate Golden, whose surgical team had been attached to the 59th Field Hospital in Boulay. The 59th supported the Yankee Division. Needless to say, Andy was elated. As it happened, I got a Paris pass in the next day or so and I stopped in Boulay to see the finance officer for my pay. Naturally I also tracked Kate down for a short bull session. She and Andy were planning great things for when the battalion got relieved the following week. However, the 59th moved out before Andy had a chance to see her. They had to be content with phone calls.

The enemy pillboxes behind the town could fire down most streets and spray the intersections. This meant each trip for a casualty had its own little portion of the big, exciting picture.

Lieutenant Golden and Lieutenant Marshall in Perlé. Photo courtesy of Ann Hall Marshall.

Each time the drivers came back they would swear that they would never make *that* run again, but they were soon back, pitching in, and taking even greater risks. Once past the relative safety of the battalion CP, we used the brakes sparingly.

We were content to get to the company CPs (which were usually located about a block back from the platoon CPs and outposts) in one piece. In fact, we jeeped right up to the company CPs, albeit using full throttle and all the requisite precautions. Waryasz once got mixed up and had his jeep forward, out in front of some tanks that were parked just this side of no-man's land. He was perplexed that the Germans would have fired on him as he crossed that intersection. We patiently explained where he had been. First he was scared, then mad, for battalion had informed him that the route was rough, but passable.

CHAPTER 13

Booze and High Jinks

THEN THERE WAS THE TIME that I went along with one of the litter squads. We jeeped to Baker CP, then ran like hell to the platoon CP where the casualties were supposed to be. Being a noble-hearted soul, I decided to carry the flag with the big red cross, just in case the Heinies were in a good mood. In case they were otherwise, we took along a Baker rifleman as a guide and guard. My .45 didn't enter the picture; I forgot all about it—probably scared. We ducked through a couple of backyards into the cellar where the platoon CP was located.

Here were several litter cases with several more reported in the yard across the street; the Heinies had fired on Mickey Fulmer and MacPherson when they tried to reach these isolated chaps. The platoon lieutenant suggested we hoist my big flag and go after the wounded men. Since I was not looking for a Purple Heart that day and could see little sense in further burdening our evacuators with my big carcass, I told our men that they were welcome to have a go at the job, but that they would do so without me. We ended up evacuating the casualties on hand.

Upon reflection, I wonder why the lieutenant didn't get busy and oust the Heinies, if he was so damn anxious about his wounded. For that, matter, why did he pull back, leaving wounded behind?

We waited a few minutes before starting, as some artillery and mortar fire was landing a couple of houses over. When it lifted, we took off, with me waving the big flag, leading a single litter (the second litter case followed on foot, for we told him either to follow us on foot or wait until we got back). I soon forgot all about the litter I was escorting and was traveling hell-bent for election through the backyards and down the street. Al Daigle, who was carrying one end of the litter hollered at me to come back, which I did, somewhat sheepishly. From then on, I traveled at the bearers' pace. We loaded the wounded onto the jeep at the company CP and screwed.

Another night Baker called in some casualties. I relayed the call back up to Battalion where Vella was manning the collecting point. I called Battalion in about twenty minutes to check and discovered Vella was still there. I blew my cheese and told Vella to get moving. I didn't know that Joe had asked for a guide to Baker, but the only Baker man present didn't know how to get to his CP. Joe had been scouting about, trying to get another guide or at least some information. When I bawled him out over the phone, he got mad, saying to hell with everything, he'd find Baker CP personally if it was the last thing he did. Sure enough, in about fifteen minutes Joe showed up at the station in his jeep with the casualty. We both laughed over the deal when we realized what had been going on.

We had artificial moonlight at Saarlautern: a huge searchlight in the rear pointed up at the clouds over German-held territory. It must have been a couple of miles behind us, but lit up the streets fairly well on dark nights. I should have written some lyrics, beginning, "Turn on the moon," but I was not in a lyric-writing mood during our stay in that city.

At the end of the first week I took off on a pass for Paris. The station reported business as usual while I was gone. The climax was furnished by an Able GI who discharged a bazooka in a cellar full of soldiers. They tell me he made a bloody mess of the place. Somehow or another it seemed our men worked out on themselves when they weren't busy with the enemy.

This bazooka incident was definitely not a deliberate SIW business—the real SIWs always aimed for the little toe of the left foot (or the right foot if they were left-handed). I was always for letting the SIWs make their own way back to the station, but Andy would get softhearted and send the jeep after them.

I returned to Hargarten from Paris Monday night where I was greeted by a batch of Mama's sugar donuts. A couple of the men were installed in Mama and Papa's barroom with the rest expected later that evening or the next morning. All arrived safely. No sooner had we settled down than we got word that we were to move to Überherrn. We were still to be held in reserve, but the move mostly cost us another crack at Mama's baking.

Our new setup was good. We had two complete houses for the medics, both in good condition. The civilians had been evacuated to one side of the railroad tracks, while we GIs were on the other. We continued on the hot meal schedule, bringing the food from the kitchen in containers and serving it family style in our own kitchen. In addition, both Vella and Cacchia had a turn at whipping up a spaghetti dinner, and each outdid the other.

For amusement we had Abie Interest and his movie projector holding forth in the local theatre every other night. Father Bransfield and the other chaplains held a sort of retreat in what was the best-looking Catholic church I had seen here so far. It was large, light paint inside, statuary neither too numerous nor gaudy in contrast with the village churches we had seen.

We used our portable shower in one of the two kitchens, enjoying hot showers at will. I found a garage suitable for a short pistol range and was kept happy and out of trouble.

One night Andy broke out the bottles; our men then proceeded to empty them. Only a few of the more rowdy characters got drunk, while the more conservative stopped at the "confiding" line. I was stuck in the middle. Andy and Valiga were singing Russian songs, Cacchia and Bruegge were for being bosom buddies with one and all, while Herbie—who had come back to us in Saarlautern—was in rare form. Another night, we talked Herbie (who was well toasted) into taking a German "prisoner" whom we had "captured," down to the CP. He borrowed my pistol (which I had unloaded) and was hustling the "PW." He practically had him out the door before he discovered the "prisoner" was really Vella, who had put on a discarded German uniform we found in the house and a Heinie helmet.

CHAPTER 14

Piercing the Siegfried Line

WE LEFT ÜBERHERRN March 5, headed north. On the way out of town, driving blackout, we rear-ended a jeep ahead of us that had stopped suddenly. The damage was minimal, but before we could get out of our jeep, a truck following us plowed into it and wrecked it thoroughly. Cacchia was scratched in the head, but that was the extent of personnel damage. The night was rainy and miserable. I climbed in the truck and we stopped in the next town to tell Service Company[1] of the wreck. We decided to stay there till morning.

In the meantime, Andy had switched from the jeep to the ambulance to follow the convoy; good thing that he did, for a QM truck packed with Baker Company soldiers overturned. The casualties were evacuated to an engineer aid station in the next town.

Meanwhile, day had come as we continued north to Serrig, which we reached by crossing the Saar River on pontoon bridges. The 94th Division and the 5th Ranger Battalion had furnished the bridges, and a rough job it must have been, for the Siegfried Line ran right along the east bank. At this point I would say that there was a pillbox right on the riverbank every couple hundred yards. Our job was to relieve the 94th and begin pushing back south

---

1. Service Company was tasked with vehicle maintenance. It was also responsible for ferrying supplies and assisting in the evacuation of the wounded.

An M10 Tank Destroyer crossing the Saar on a newly constructed pontoon bridge, December 1944. Courtesy of Wikimedia Commons.

along the east bank, right through the heart of the Siegfried Line. Thank heavens we would be coming down its flank instead of hitting it head-on. Apparently the Germans neglected this angle when they built the fortifications.

We stopped in Serrig for only a few hours, then moved out to effect the relief. The battalion was to establish a holding position in the woods about four kilometers east of the town. The 94th Division had their aid station in Serrig, but we decided to move east up a draw in which the battalion CP was located. We discovered a large cave in the draw, manmade, consisting of a tunnel eight feet high and eight feet wide that ran back to a room that was fifteen feet high, thirty feet long, and twenty feet wide. I don't know what the Heinies used it for, but it suited our needs pretty well. It was damp but safe. We had to use lights all the time and heating was a problem we never did solve; we tried a gasoline-powered kitchen stove, but it burned the oxygen out. We couldn't get enough stovepipe to run a pot-bellied stove.

Getting to the companies was tough. They were all up in the woods on top of the hills around us, but roads were nonexistent. The trails were muddy and steep, so every time we started out, it was an open question whether we would reach our objective or get stuck in the muck. At first, Able occupied a position considerably off to the left. A fairly decent trail led up the draw and the hillside to their CP. We asked the 94th about this trail, and they said they had never used it, but that it had been swept of enemy mines.

Before we could give it a try, the wire jeep took the initiative and started up it. Soon everybody was hollering the old familiar "medic!" for the jeep had struck a mine. The jeep was blown a good twenty yards off the trail, but the only injury was a badly gashed face; the GI had been hit by a piece of the jeep after he had been thrown clear. The A & P boys swept the road, finding a couple more American mines in the area where the jeep had come a cropper. The 94th had cleaned the road of enemy mines, but apparently had substituted some of our own and neglected to mention it.

A couple of farms and plenty of cleared space were at the top of the hill where Able was located, so after one night in the cave and a run to Able after casualties, we decided to split the station, setting half of it in one of the farmhouses. We fixed the place up in the afternoon and left a couple of men there for the night, intending to make the move up in the morning. I was looking forward to moving along with this section, but a change of Able's position was ordered in the morning, so all bets were off. The company was to shift right to contact Baker, so our whole plan— road and all—fell through.

This change of positions was amusing for the fact that our old buddy, Jackson Kahner, had set up his light machine guns so that they would be firing right into Baker's outposts. (Jackson had managed to stagger back after each of his previous evacuations.) Luckily his error was discovered before the guns were fired. I would be inclined to say that this was typical of Jackson, except that the truth is nobody seemed to know where anybody else was half the time.

The Germans managed to lob an occasional shell into our positions, causing a few casualties. Indeed, we went tearing up the hill one day to find Kahner had been wounded by shrapnel.

It was more than a scratch, but still not serious. We packed him back down and sent him off in the ambulance. That was the last we ever saw of Jackson Kahner, one-time battalion S-2 and platoon leader extraordinaire!

We also lost one of our best medics at this time—Mac McPherson was killed by a shell as Dog Company was moving up the draw past a vineyard to take its initial positions on the first day.

A little creek ran between the mouth of our cave and the road up the draw, so it was necessary for us medics to turn engineer. We produced a very substantial footbridge. About this time the anti-tank crew came along with their guns and settled into a cave next to ours. They had to park their guns on the other side of the creek, and did so in such a manner that it looked as if they were intended to cover the approaches to our bridge. We felt honored in a way that two 57-mm anti-tank guns should be guarding our "bridgehead" and we let the entire battalion know about it. Our one regret was that Tony Geydos was not around to get his share of the razzing.

To my knowledge these guns had been fired in combat only once—at Bezange, yet we dragged them around with us religiously. Personally, I think we should have dumped the guns in a river and used their trucks to haul rations—either that or fire them occasionally if only to shoot the rust out of the barrels.

When Watkins and the others returned from their night up on the hill in the farmhouse, they considerately brought along some of that farmyard delicacy, chicken on the hoof, which we soon translated with the help of the Able kitchen (located back in Serrig) into chicken à la frying pan. Very tasty morsels, they were. It was in our cave that I almost lost my pants in a poker game. It took me four months to get all my IOUs from that fatal night paid off, but I was at last convinced that I wasn't a poker player.

The regimental CP was set up in the castle back in Serrig. They must have been as happy there as we were unhappy in our damp cave—short-lived happiness, for along came the division CP chaps and ousted them from the castle (RHIP: rank has its privileges). Father Bransfield happened by one day to say Mass, and insisted on celebrating it in the cave, though the day was bright and pleasant enough for a field Mass outside. I think he may have imagined our cave to resemble the catacombs of old Rome and wanted a bit of local color. This is perhaps a little snide of me to say, for the good pater was certainly on the beam when it came to religious services for us 1st Battalion medics.

The regiment was poised in the woods up on the hills east and south of Serrig, ready to drive down the east bank of the Saar toward Saarlautern. The 1st Battalion was to be in regimental reserve, so the day before the jump-off, the battalion pulled back to an assembly area just south of the big vineyard. We found an intact pillbox that the Heinies may have used, among other things, for some sort of medical purpose, so thither we moved from the cave on March 11 or 12.

Lieutenant Marshall in a jeep *on top of* a pillbox at Serrig. RTM notes on the original picture, "The ventilator can be seen by the left rear wheel." Photo courtesy of Ann Hall Marshall.

About this time, we switched battalion COs—Colonel Menard came back to take Major Parriot's place. The latter had been evacuated with a genuine case of yellow jaundice. I say "genuine," for about this same time Colonel Hamilton was railroaded out of the regimental CO spot by the brass, who told MacKillop to send Hamilton back with a diagnosis of yellow jaundice. He was a good man, but I suppose he stepped on some higher-up's toes and out he went. Colonel O'Flaherty replaced him, and though I am half Irish, I say with fervency that we lost in the exchange. Cacchia also left us while we were still in the cave—sinus trouble as a result of the jeep accident at Überherrn.

The pillbox was a relief after the cave—dry and warm. We had nothing to do but enjoy life, for there were no casualties the first couple of days. The pillbox was on a steep slope with the companies farther up the hill, so we were able to park the jeep on top of the fortification to drive on up if necessary. It was a novel sight to see the jeep sitting on top of the station. We climbed around the vineyard, and visited the chateau where the slave laborers who worked the place had been kept.

When Herbie Scheinberg came north from Jackson to Camp Shanks on the train, the city boy, seeing the Statue of Liberty for the first time from another angle, thought that it had been turned around. The same city boy saw a couple of young deer bouncing across a nearby field and expressed great wonderment to see the "rabbits" go by. Watkins and Melnicoff grabbed an M1 and went after these unusually large "rabbits," but had no luck.

CHAPTER 15

Army Politics

ONCE WE BEGAN OUR PUSH, all hell broke loose. Transportation was quite a problem for a day or two. We made one run up into the woods to reconnoiter and brought some casualties back for the 2d Battalion; the round trip took a couple of hours. After we were committed, we had fewer casualties than the other battalions. Captain Meade of Baker finally went down for the count when he stepped on a shoe mine, though his injury was not fatal.

After such a long jeep haul, we started to investigate the river road on March 14. From the road we found a trail leading up the side of the mountain to the general area of the fighting, so the next morning we moved into a railroad station along the river on the east bank, across from Hamm. The trail wasn't much of an improvement over those we had been using, but it cut the length of the haul by a couple of miles.

We were expecting plenty of action that morning, so we assembled all the company cooks from Serrig in the aid station. Along with some of our own men, we set them up on top of the hill in the woods at a collecting point in a large, abandoned Heine dugout. Our concern was unfounded for we had no casualties that day or night. The troops had pushed quite a distance, getting as far as a hunting lodge a kilometer or so north of Saarhölzbach.

The next morning, we found a much better road running up the hill across from Tauben.[1] By noon we had the collecting point in the lodge, by nightfall we had the entire station in Saarhölzbac. Indeed, things were going very well—witness the fact that we got into town barely ahead of the regimental CP, which was always very cautious about sticking their necks out.

Saturday morning, March 17, we headed south toward Mettlach and Merzig. Instead of following the troops who were going through the woods, we thought we'd pull a fast one, get back down to the river road, and head south that way. Orlovich, Daigle, German, and I piled into the jeep and started out to reconnoiter. Shortly after we left Saarhölzbac, we found the road blown, but the railroad that ran parallel to the road between it and the river was still intact.

We started down the tracks on foot to see if we might be able to swing the vehicles around the crater in the road by means of the railroad that ran through a cut, which in turn shielded the railroad from the river. Walt German, noticing some pine branches piled against a rock as if concealing something, pulled them aside. We almost fainted dead away, for there was a live German soldier having his morning piss. The branches con-

---

1. Taben-Rodt.

cealed a sort of cave or passageway running through the rock and forming a rear entrance to one of the many riverside pill-boxes. As usual, I forgot all about my gun. We began to talk fast, telling this guy how he was hopelessly surrounded by tanks, infantry, and so on. The only reason nobody had appeared here so far was that everybody was too busy heading for Germany and capturing larger formations. Between us and our fractured Deutsch we got the general idea across that surrendering would be the smart thing to do. He was perfectly agreeable and maintained that he had intended to surrender all along.

Next he hollered down the passage and behold, after a minute or two, out came five more Heinies. Since their philosophy of war and defeat matched their buddy's, we started back to town with our six captives. We deposited them with the first GIs we ran into—the motor maintenance gang—and headed down the road again, for by this time the engineers had bulldozed the crater roadblock. We were able to get the jeep into Mettlach with little trouble. But getting out of Mettlach in the direction we wanted to go was another matter—the roads leading south and east were effectively cratered and logged.[2] We finally turned back.

Next we took all the men and vehicles and began to follow the route that the battalion had taken. It wasn't exactly cross-country for us, for we were able to swing back and forth along roads and trails. On one of these swings, we picked up another Heine prisoner. Seeing the red cross on our vehicles, he must have decided that we were good people to surrender to.

On another swing we lost the battalion completely. About this time, Lt. Dick Irwin (wounded at Bezange, but now back taking Geydos' place) came along, joining Andy and me in our search for the battalion. We were in the woods somewhere east of Mettlach, and none of our compatriots were to be seen. We drove back and forth for an hour or so, up one trail and down another; there were GIs all over the place, but no Handcar Red GIs.

---

2. The retreating enemy had rendered the roads impassable by leaving hasty obstacles in their wake to slow the pursuit.

A drawing of the jeep with wire cutter described by Marshall and in footnote 3. Photo, public domain, courtesy of Aden Nichols.

I was at the wheel and almost got Andy killed by driving under a telephone wire that was draped loosely across the road. I must have ducked and our wire cutter[3] must have missed it somehow, for it caught Andy across the neck. I jammed on the brakes; all I could see was a black bruise line across his throat where the wire hit. His head was still attached, but that black line made me think his goose was cooked. Fortunately, the wire had been quite slack and had given enough, so in the end all Andy had to show for it was a generous welt, a sore neck, and a Purple Heart.

We were becoming disgusted with ourselves and our efforts at scouting when, turning up a trail, we bumped into Lieutenants Warrick, Skeels, and Arrington, and some enlisted men. They announced breathlessly that they had just seen a couple of Heinie

3. Late in the war, jeeps and other open vehicles were fitted with an improvised device (essentially a vertical iron bar, several feet tall, affixed to the front bumper) to catch and deflect taut wire booby traps.

disappear into a hole up ahead and decided to screw. More foolishly than intelligently, we announced sweetly that if the infantry was afraid of Heinies, the medics were not. As we started along up the trail, Warrick decided to come with us. The others then turned about and followed sheepishly.

Sure enough, we shortly came across two German 15-cm howitzers[4] set up in firing position. With a little prompting, two Heinies crawled out of a nearby dugout and surrendered. The S-2 reports that night mentioned the fact that the regiment had overrun an enemy artillery battery, taking both guns and crew intact. Of course, the reports failed to mention that we 1st Battalion medics had done the overrunning and capturing, but then it would have looked bad for the infantry and for Skeels, who, as S-2, probably drafted said report.

When we finally got to Merzig, we found the battalion setting up for the night; we did likewise. An interesting town, it looked at first as if it had good looting possibilities, but upon examination it seemed that the Germans had done the job themselves after evacuating the civilians. We found some canned sardines in a pillbox in the backyard of the house we had picked for the station, and these constituted the sum total of our loot. Andy and I went looking for a hospital and a microscope, but wound up in a jewelry store that already had been rifled. It had been a strenuous day, so there was little more to do except grab some chow and hit the sack. The menu featured 10-in-1 rations.[5]

---

4. There were three 15-cm artillery pieces in the German inventory: the sFH 18 (*schwere Feldhaubitze 18*); the K 18 (*Kanone 18*); and the sIG 33 (*schweres Infanterie Geschütz 33*). Marshall probably encountered the last of these, as the sIG 33 was the standard front-line heavy infantry gun.

5. The 10-in-1 ration was intended for issue primarily to mechanized troops or those with a crew-type organization. They were a consolidated daily ration designed to serve ten soldiers a varied menu of breakfast, a midday snack, and supper meals. A typical menu included such canned items as a meat dish, vegetables, margarine, and pudding, along with cereal, biscuits, jam, and of course, coffee. Accessory items included chewing gum, cigarettes and matches, a can opener, toilet paper, soap, towels, and water purification tablets.

Sunday morning's program called for a move to Düppenweiler, which was accomplished almost without incident. We had been following Dog Company vehicles, not paying much attention to where we were going. The first thing we knew, they had lost the rest of the column; we wound up in Haustadt, where the bridge had been blown. We took the lead, swung back and up through Honzrath, and into Düppenweiler.

Mumme had given us the usual second-rate quarters, so we scouted around and found an empty doctor's house. The doc had absconded, but his women folk (who were still in residence) put up a howl when they heard they were to have company for the night. One old lady spoke English; she was very solicitous as to whether women and children would be safe in the same house with our own laddies. We slipped her the old Shermanism about war and hell and all that baloney. We also told her to feel free to pack up and leave any time she desired. The town was beaten up pretty badly, so the resident women and children decided to take their chances with the 1st Battalion medics.

I got no complaints about rape, robbery, or romance when we left the next morning, though it seems somebody lifted all the eggs in the vicinity. The men had been sore as hell at me that night for decreeing that we post a guard over the vehicles. Not being fond of walking, though, I couldn't bear the thought of sabotaged tires and the like, so the guard went on, grumbling notwithstanding.

Around noon the next day we loaded up and headed north. We rolled into Framersheim around dusk. While en route, we speculated that we were headed first for Worms, then for Bingen. A nice feature of our race for the Rhine was that we never knew our immediate destinations. Somebody obviously did, but we were never able to contact said somebody. Another example: The day before, we thought we were headed for Speyer or Ludwigzhafen.

The entrance into Framersheim was a real triumphal affair. Someone had let it slip that the town would be burned if the roadblocks leading out of the village were not removed before dark. From the way we came belting and hollering into the place, I imagine we appeared to be just the sort of laddies to do such a thing.

We medics found a comfortable house that belonged to one of the local Nazis and we made ourselves at home. It was a big house with a bathroom with running hot water, so we all had a bath. After the night before, which we spent on a living room carpet, we prepared to enjoy this night between real sheets in beds. I rummaged around and found some silk nightclothes to wear; although there was much discussion as to whether they were intended for a male or female, they were clean, so they were fine by me.

Frank Valiga heated up some 10-in-1s for our supper and we hit the sack. In the morning, Father Bransfield showed up and celebrated Mass in the local church. We acquired and lost (in the space of an hour) a lovely truck that would have made an "Aid Station on Wheels." An order came from on high to turn in all non-GI vehicles to Service Company, which by some miracle happened to be in Framersheim. I took the truck down to see if an exception couldn't be made for us, but Major Young—regimental S-4 and a mean-spirited sort—started to get nasty, about what, I don't know. So we left the truck in his backyard. Then, as it happened, he turned the truck over to Tony DeVito for his dental equipment. That is what is known as "army politics."

CHAPTER 16

"Keep 'Em Rolling!"

THURSDAY AFTERNOON, March 22, we headed north again, destination unknown. After a short ride, we sat along the road for about four hours. Then our unknown "somebody" decided we would stay in Stadecken for the night. A railroad station and warehouse stood on the outskirts of that town where the troops were to sleep in the fields. Military government had managed to catch up to us in time to decree that the poor German citizens of Stadecken couldn't be expected to make room in their homes for GIs at that hour of night. (Though the GIs could be expected to pitch tents and sleep on the ground.) We opted to sleep in the warehouse and set the aid station up in the train station. The warehouse was an unhappy choice, for what we took to be sacks of grain turned out to be unground, black pepper. We sneezed our way outside, took slabs of corrugated paper, and spread our bedrolls out under the stars.

No sooner were we comfortable than that damned "somebody" put us on the move again.

In the wee hours of the next morning, we pulled into a German barracks at the east end of Gonsenheim, and again tried for some sleep. We pulled the barracks beer hall/PX for quarters, but the 90th Division GIs had given the place a good going over, so the pickings were slim. Knives and stationery were all that was available. However, I found two footlockers in the basement belonging to a Heinie *hauptmann*[1] full of clothes and such. I snagged a bathrobe for myself.

Bright and early came the dawn and the news that we were at the wrong end of town—we belonged back with battalion CP, so back we went. This time we had a large house, but no electricity or running water. Its furnishings showed the occupants to be very well-to-do, for there was not one, but *two* baby grand pianos, good carpets, books, a couple of phonographs with records, and similar trappings of high social status. We were here a couple of days. The troops were in Mainz, of which Gonsenheim was a suburb.

Civilians still remained in these parts. In our residential section most of them seemed as affluent as our involuntary hosts. When Mumme rousted the inhabitants out of the co-opted CP, the lady of the house informed him that the Americans were "cruel." Very ironical, for probably such moneyed and professional people were the very backers and backbone of the Nazi Party and the war. Mumme told her so in so many words and continued the rousting. We medics had no problems with our civilians.

Life in Gonsenheim was pleasant. The weather was just right—plenty of warm sunshine in which we reveled. Both phonographs were put to work. One of the cooks came over one evening to give the pianos a workout. Andy, forgetting himself, let loose on a bottle and became a bit tipsy. He ended up trying to organize a combat patrol against some TD outposts down the street from us and almost ripped off Arrington's ear when he wouldn't cooperate. We slipped him a Mickey Finn to settle him for the evening.

We had no casualties while here. Denny and I made a run into Mainz to look the place over and to see what might be available in the line of alcohol. The city was really a wreck—we were told that it was the result of a single air raid that lasted only an

---

1. Captain.

hour. Almost every building showed some damage, while most were either empty shells or piles of rubble. On the whole, the troops were quartered on the first floors of apartment buildings that were still in some kind of shape.

Lieutenant Toomey of Dog Company took us visiting to a wine cellar that would have done Poe and his *Cask of Amontillado* proud. There were the interminable steps down to the dank, dungeon-like vaults where the wine and champagne were racked in bottles and casks. We took a load of the stuff back to supplement our brandy. We also got some canned fruit for snacks. During this visit I got my first glimpse of the Rhine. Charlie Company was in an apartment house a block from the water, so Lieutenant Moise took me over to see the storied river. An island in midstream was supposedly being held by some dug-in Germans, while snipers were said to be firing from the buildings on the opposite bank. However, as we stood on the bank and looked across, all was serene.

Palm Sunday, Father Bransfield said Mass on the street corner near the battalion CP, using a soft drink stand for an altar. Late that afternoon we were relieved by a cavalry group. Loading up, we headed south through Mainz to the village of Lörzweiler. All the way down we could see the antiaircraft tracers streaming up through the dusk around the bridgehead site. When we got to the village, the real show began with parachute flares bright as a full moon and tracers by the thousands. We could even make out a riding light on one of the attacking enemy planes—well, it was either a light or a hit, but if the latter, the plane managed to escape.

Shortly after midnight we left Lörzweiler headed for the Rhine. After the usual wrong turns, one of which we repeated and made a second time, we got into Oppenheim on the river. We crossed on a pontoon bridge east of the city. Driving through the village of Leeheim, we saw the still-smoldering vehicles that the night's bombing had left. It was the first time I had seen the immediate results of enemy bombing and it left an odd feeling in my throat. We stopped in Wolfskehlen for breakfast and a few hours' rest. Waryasz went egg hunting in the barn behind the house where we were staying and found a Heinie soldier hiding in the hay.

From Wolskehlen we went through Darmstadt and headed northeast. That city was bombed even worse than Mainz, but I remember it because here we saw our illustrious division general, General Paul, for the second time, and his inspirational words were, to be exact, "Keep 'em rolling!"

We heard that the regiment's mission was to support Combat Command B of the 4th Armored; they had grabbed an intact railroad bridge across the Mainz River at Grossauheim, but lacked the necessary troops to hold and exploit their bridgehead. We stopped short in Hainstadt to get organized. We watched our Thunderbolts work over Hanau, while the Heinies returned the compliment with some excellently timed fire.[2] It looked as though they were using antiaircraft rifles as regular artillery. They were getting airbursts at rooftop height over Grossauheim.

We had displaced the civilians from our (their) house and were making ourselves comfortable when we found that we had another move to make before dark, this time to the companion town of Klein-Auheim. The troops were going on across the river at Grossauheim. Once more, we moved the civilians out of their house and started to settle in for the night. I had just crawled into my sleeping bag, when in came Irwin with the news that he was going to take me on a reconnaissance trip across the river to the battalion forward CP and the companies. I gave up on rest for that night.

---

2. Artillery fire employing projectiles armed with timed fuses so they would detonate prior to impact, thus maximizing the antipersonnel effect of the shrapnel.

CHAPTER 17

Yours Truly
Gets Blown Up

GROSSAUHEIM WAS COMPARATIVELY QUIET, but it was a long haul from here back to the aid station, so we ended up moving the station across the river. By the time we got there it was after midnight. We settled down for the rest of the night and managed to make it stick. We had profited by the exchange of quarters, for while our house in Klein-Auheim hadn't been much to speak of, our new building was much like the one we had enjoyed in Gonsenheim.

The occupants had taken to the cellar, but rather than evict them, after a thorough search we opted to let them stay. We took over the entire upstairs of this commodious dwelling. The morning showed our choice to be a good one. The man of the house was apparently a buyer for a store of some sort, for the place was loaded with statuary, stationery, clothes, and so on. I don't know what his grown daughter did for a living, but her dresser drawers had quite a supply of rubber prophylactics.

I was rousted out of bed by a timed burst like the ones we had been seeing from across the river. While it didn't send any shrapnel in my window, it did blow the shutter off and killed the CP guard standing in a doorway across the street. We had other casualties during the night, which the men picked up without incident. The day also brought us two Heinie wounded and one French casualty.

This was Wednesday, March 28. Shortly after lunch, Father Bransfield came around and said Mass for us in the cellar. The companies had moved slowly northeast all day, then turned back west from Wolfgang toward Hanau.

Outside of Wolfgang, they ran into a Heinie OCS school of some sort and captured about seven hundred prisoners. About suppertime, Colonel Menard decided to go over to Wolfgang to see about moving the battalion CP there. Madden, Daigle, Orlovich, and I trailed along in our jeep to see where the companies were and suss out what was going on. Halfway there we encountered some riflemen carrying Ingrassia, an aidman who had been clipped in the testicles. Bad luck, that. We took him back and headed for Wolfgang once more.

The large haul of prisoners made an inspiring sight, all lined up and marching to the rear. Baker Company was still in town, while Able and Charlie had already started for Hanau. Orlovich and Daigle took a couple of slightly wounded GIs and some Heinie wounded back, while Madden and I scouted around the village looking for a house. We found a suitable place that proved to be inhabited by a distinguished old gent sporting a wing collar. We told him to expect us back soon, and went to check in with the colonel. Menard reported that he had discovered that there was a gap between our right flank and the left flank of the 101st, and not wanting to leave us exposed, he had decided not to move up after all.

We were starting back when the colonel asked us to haul a Heinie prisoner Denny had spotted and the boys from Charlie had scooped up. We sat him on the hood and started back in the gathering dusk. To the right of the road was a wooded area, to the left an open field. We saw tanks moving toward us up the road and turning off into the field as we approached. But the lead tank kept coming. Someone was hollering like mad and trying to wave us down. The next thing we knew, there was a terrific blast and we all went sailing through the air.

At first I thought that the TC[1] had mistaken us for Germans and let go with his cannon; however, when I came to, I was told that a Heinie who had been hiding in the woods heard the tanks coming and sneaked out to put some Teller mines[2] on the road. Due to the limited visibility, we had been headed right for the mines. The tanker realized this, and had deliberately driven over them to prevent us from doing so. The blast blew a tread off his tank, and it showered us with bits and pieces of shredded steel.

Judging from the amount of blood all over my face, I thought I was dying, but I was pleasantly surprised to find that I could open my eyes and breathe. Madden was hollering that both his legs were broken. Fred Orlovich was lying there yelling, "Save me, Lieutenant Marshall! Save me, I'm dying!"

"Fred," I replied gallantly, "I can't save you, I'm dying myself!"

A 4th Armored medic trotted up and administered first aid to Orlovich and Madden. Colonel Menard soon appeared and hauled the lot of us back to the aid station in his jeep.

That was the end of the road for me; that affair put me out of action until well after VE Day. Amidst all the brouhaha, I can't seem to recall what happened to our prisoner. Poor bloke hitched a ride on the wrong jeep.

---

1. Tank commander.
2. The German word *teller* means dish or plate, a reference to the physical appearance of these anti-tank mines. The teller mine comprised a hubcap-sized sheet metal casing packed with about twelve pounds of TNT that was detonated by a pressure-activated fuse. It was simple and extremely effective, and Germany produced them by the millions.

Staff Sgt. Walter German, author of next 2 chapters.
Photo courtesy of the German family.

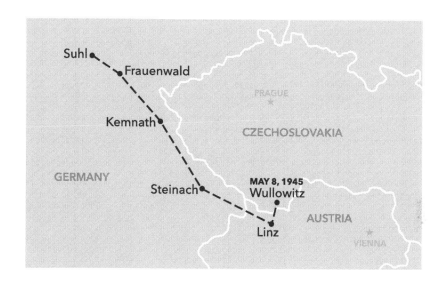

CHAPTER 18

Widowmakers

Editor's note: After his wounding, Lieutenant Marshall became a participant in the aforementioned "chain of evacuation." He and his comrades received treatment for their wounds by a medic on the scene, and were then transported to the very aid station they had set up earlier that day at Grossauheim. From there, Marshall was sent back to a field hospital, and it would be a month before he had recuperated sufficiently to rejoin his unit.

At this point in the narrative, S. Sgt. Walter German picks up the story.

During our stay in the battered city of Hanau,[1] Captain Dedick and I stumbled onto a paradise of sorts: a well-appointed German station hospital that had been evacuated completely by the Heinies! Although it had been somewhat damaged by Allied bombing, all of the surgical instruments and drugs were intact, so we immediately took advantage of this unexpected windfall. We exited from the hospital toting two brand new microscopes complete with slides and all of the other auxiliary equipment. As we turned to leave, our interest was drawn to a large warehouse and we strolled over to investigate.

Our already perfect day just got better when we found that the warehouse was full of foods of all kinds. When we returned to our aid station about two or three hours later, we were really stuffed and our jeep was laden with these delicious edibles, so the feast was on. It was too bad our wounded men couldn't share in this repast with us, but we certainly enjoyed ourselves—so much, in fact, that the arrival of our new MAC officer, Lieutenant Adee, went almost unnoticed. He just grabbed a jar of fruit from the table and dove in. Later, the formal introduction was made. He came to us from Baker Company of the medical battalion (the collecting company that handled casualties from the 104th Regiment). The Germans really furnished us with a pleasant evening meal this time.

We departed from Hanau with still slightly dampened spirits in the absence of our four aid station compatriots: Lieutenant Marshall, Dennis Madden, Albert Daigle, and Fred Orlovitch.

After a short ride to the east, we rolled into Wolfgang and paused for a bit while the doughs flushed a patch of nearby woods. Suddenly all hell broke loose in those treacherous woods,

---

1. The city of Hanau was pummeled by British bombers on March 19, 1945, only days before its inevitable fall to the advancing U.S. Army. Its railway junction had also been bombed in early January, with the city center suffering 40 percent damage; this run took that number up to 85 percent. The 328th met stiff resistance in its attempt to clear the town, fighting house to house. The GIs secured the town on March 28, capturing 1,100 Germans in the process.

and casualties began to pour into the aid station like crazy. We quickly set up in a battered house and sent our two cooks into the kitchen to begin preparation of coffee and the evening meal. When we got into a hot situation, nothing served to calm our nerves like a steaming mug of joe. Time after time, these hasty meals whipped up by Frank Valiga and Harry Winner, coupled with our officers' steadiness, saved us from cracking up from combat fatigue. While the cooks worked in the kitchen, we made a reconnaissance of our proposed evacuation routes to the companies.

An advance aid station was set up within five hundred yards of the front lines to facilitate the speedy treatment of the wounded. This policy had been followed in all similar situations; by rotating advanced station personnel every twelve hours, we achieved excellent results. For the next three days we really worked our butts off. Three more medics—Myles Fulmer, Jack Reed, and Roberto Rios—had to be evacuated, all with slight wounds. After this ordeal, we all needed a rest; the companies were far understrength (with only about three hundred men left in the entire

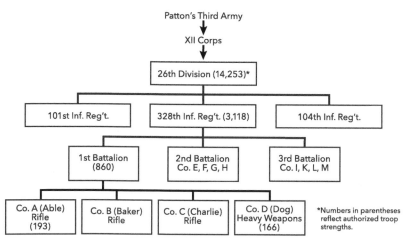

A representation of the numbers of troops typically assigned to various military units. Illustration courtesy of Aden Nichols.

battalion[2]); the medics were exhausted, and our new MAC liaison was just learning the ropes.

Fighting in the woods is grim. Not only must a man endure the fury and the firepower of the German infantry, he must also contend with the terrible effectiveness of the constant barrages of timed artillery shells exploding overhead in the treetops. This type of barrage threw white-hot shrapnel in all directions with terrific force. From our medical perspective, we feared all wooded areas—they always provided us with plenty of customers.

On April 2, we finally received some rest by becoming a reserve regiment for a combat team from the 11th Armored Division. After riding for several hours through a very cold German night, our motorized column stopped in a small town for what was supposed to be only a few moments. Those few moments dragged on into long hours and the night got uncomfortably colder. We were so cold that sleep was impossible; the situation had to be remedied but quick. George Trabucco and John Waryasz found a simple solution—they pounded on the door of a nearby house and an old woman opened it. In trooped the entire gang and within five minutes we had a brisk fire roaring and the coffee percolating.

We stayed in that kitchen until morning, at which time we continued on to Untenbinbach[3] in much better spirits. We had just settled down to a life of ease to begin relaxing, cleaning the thick layer of red German mud from our clothing, and scraping the whiskers off our dreary mugs, when word was received of another supposed calamity. A pocket of German soldiers who had been bypassed and left in our rear by the swiftly moving

---

2. Per Army Strength Key, Figure 15, the authorized strength of the First Battalion was 860 men.
3. German place names can be confusing. From March 28–April 4, the 328th Infantry was engaged in clearing a number of towns, working its way northeast from Hanau through Rückingen (March 30), Büdingen (March 31), and Grossenlüder (April 1). The regiment then turned east and swept through Fulda and towns to its north (April 3–4). "Untenbinbach" is a reference to the village of Unterbimbach, which is just south of Grossenlüder on the highway to Fulda.

columns of armor and infantry suddenly erupted into trouble. Being the reserve combat team, we were naturally called upon to remedy the situation. The griping began immediately because we knew that another division, the 71st, was much closer to the scene than we were and could neutralize the menace more easily. But the 71st Division was green, so this was one time when battle experience hurt us more than it helped. Still bitching loudly, we loaded up and hightailed it down to within a few miles of Hintzkihn,[4] the center of the activity.

Leaving our transport parked alongside the road, I went forward with the troops and some tanks as a recon man in order to find a good house in which to set up the station. We walked into town unopposed, and after quickly tagging a likely house for our aid station, I joined the rest of the GIs in an egg-gathering mission. I went from house to house and filled all my pockets completely, very pleased by the thought of having gathered tomorrow's breakfast. But as I exited one house, I found the doughs running towards the outskirts of town and dropping into firing positions. The tanks were spinning around quickly to follow, while other men disappeared into houses and poked the barrels of their M1s through the windows in true sniper fashion. With all the hubbub, about all I could learn was that the Jerries were attacking our town and were supposed to have us surrounded! In a flash, my pockets were emptied of their precious and delicate cargo, and I was setting up a one-man aid station.

Small arms fire quickly reached a furious tempo and I really started to shake, but my spirits rose when I saw our battalion commander, Colonel Menard, walking down the street as cool as you please, directing the activities by radio. He was really a soldier's soldier.

Later in the day, the truth of the matter revealed that the Germans were not attacking; rather, they were *retreating* in all

---

4. The only town in the area that sounds remotely like "Hintzkihn" is Hirzenhain. It lies about 20 miles southwest of Unterbimbach, as the crow flies. This fits German's description, "we … hightailed it *down* to Hintzkihn" (emphasis added).

directions, and our boys were picking them off like fish in a barrel. It was April 4, 1945, and a lot of German women became widows that day.

We had the enemy on the run. After two days of steady punching, we settled down for the night far to the northeast in a small farm town called Rosa.[5] This was just the kind of situation in which our German-speaking men blossomed. There were too many GIs looking for eggs in Rosa, so Melnicoff, Watkins, and Jenkins drove out to the next little hamlet to beat the rush. They brought back more than enough eggs for both our supper and breakfast. We had about six eggs apiece—*luxury!* That night we thoroughly enjoyed our supper in our aid station site, and mapped out plans for our next day's activities.

In the morning, one jeep and four men fell in directly behind the foot troops with the full aid station following much later in the day. This proved to be the practice we followed every day from this time on. It worked out very effectively.

That night we all celebrated our brief breathing spell in a lovely private home replete with all the modern conveniences. We drained an entire keg of good German beer, accompanied by shots of American whiskey as chasers. We were living high on the hog. It was here that we changed our MAC officer again; we were now led by 1st Lt. Julius Richardson. We lived almost as civilians in this billet, sleeping in nice, soft beds, and enjoying the modern plumbing facilities and electric lights. Our electrician, Waryasz, had a radio playing in short order, so everything was jake. It certainly was disheartening to know that we would soon have to leave this cozy nest, but that was Army SOP: you pass through the nice places quickly and remain in the squalid little hamlets indefinitely.

At daybreak we were on the move again. After a rather boring day of crawling along behind the foot troops, interrupted

---

5. Rosa was captured on April 5, 1945.

once by several casualties who had fallen prey to a cleverly hidden German booby trap, we ended up on the outskirts of Suhl.[6] We knew Suhl was famous for its high-quality firearms makers,[7] so needless to say, within a half-hour of setting up the station the next day in Lauter (a small town just north of Suhl), we scattered throughout the town to scope out the workshops, trolling for souvenirs. This paid big dividends, and we all returned to the aid station with superb new shotguns, beautiful knives, and similar examples of the metal-crafter's art.

Melnicoff found a dandy .22-caliber pistol, so a session of target practice followed. Judging from the results, we agreed that we were much better qualified as combat medics than marksmen, but it was still fun. That evening we settled down to a few rubbers of bridge instead of the usual round of poker. We'd lost plenty of dough playing "baseball" (a variant of poker) in the last month, so we were satisfied with this change of pace. Captain Dedick departed for a couple of weeks' rest at regimental, and a fellow named Captain Streepey filled in for him. Streepey was a very, very cautious doctor, and he also proved to be a fair hand at bridge.

Our house in Lauter was nothing special, but had we known what the conditions would be like at our next stop, we would gladly have stayed. It was here that we had our first taste of the vengeful attitude that characterized the Nazi's slave laborers. Soon after we left, the factories were literally torn apart by hundreds of jubilant liberated people. They looted or destroyed everything within their grasp. Delicate machinery was smashed to bits; nails, tools, parts, and other rubbish littered the floors of the factories as the mass of giddy people surged onward. We

---

6. The 328th approached Suhl on April 7. The regiment assaulted the city the following morning, but met little resistance.

7. Suhl, on the northwestern edge of the Thüringian Forest (*Thüringer Wald*), had been a mining and metalworking district since the Middle Ages; it evolved into a small arms manufacturing hub by the late nineteenth century. The gun makers of Suhl thrived during WWI, and they experienced another boom in the 1930s, when their factories began to land lucrative contracts as a result of the Nazi rearmament program. During the war, those same factories were operated by slave labor.

enlisted their help for our various needs and the results were very pleasing. Perhaps we should have forbidden this wholesale ransacking, but after gazing upon the tattered clothing and hunger-lined faces, we merely turned our backs and looked the other way. The tales of brutality and cruelty they related to us turned our stomachs—truly barbarous acts of war. When we left town some two hours later, the entire place was in shambles, but after seeing the state of these slave laborers, we really didn't care.

That day's drive forward halted in the small town of Frauen-wald.[8] This huge forest furnished us with a good view of the care and efficiency the Germans applied to their woodlands. This meticulous stewardship is not pursued for the fun of it, but rather out of necessity. Woodlands in Germany are the source of fuel, shoes, furniture, and even food. Lately, they had also been the source of gunstocks. Being well aware of this fact, the shrewd Germans had diverted millions of their slave laborers to the care and preservation of their forests. One could not help but admire the neatness found in every timbered region throughout Germany. Beauty produced by cruelty. The ground was completely clear of underbrush and cords of wood were neatly stacked along the sides of the roads.

In the center of the town stood a beautiful statue of a doe and her fawn, acknowledging that the nearby woods were flush with deer. The name Frauenwald suited this town perfectly—"the women of the forest"—there were plenty of *fraus* and lots of trees, but what it lacked was eggs and other staples. About the only bright spot of our stay in this town was that we finally got our "monthly" pay. This, coupled with the view of the beautiful scenery surrounding us, made the place tolerable. This was the first time we were paid off in German invasion marks, so naturally this change was hotly debated.

---

8. Frauenwald was seized on April 10.

CHAPTER 19

Cruisin' Down the Autobahn

THE NEXT THREE DAYS were spent in constant motion up and down the hilly terrain in the midst of this beautiful but treacherous forest. Our nightly stops were made in typical small towns, such as Massenthal, Schmalkalden, and Neuhaus until we finally cleared the forest, stopping in Nordhausen.[1]

During our travels through the forest, we came across something that typified the very worst of Nazism. As we rode along one of the highways following the companies, one of our men noticed a human arm half covered with dirt off the side of the road. We stopped the jeep and called a farmer over from a nearby field for information. He related that in that crude grave lay ten Polish prisoners who had been shot in cold blood only that morning by their SS guards. We were outraged. This was what we were fighting. We were aware of the fact there was a great difference between the activities of the SS and the regular German army, the Wehrmacht; the SS were Hitler's hired gangsters, Nazis through-and-through, and they were very much hated by ordinary German civilians. Nevertheless, we hated the whole kit and caboodle!

---

1. Again, Walter German was writing after hostilities had ceased, and his military responsibilities had differed from Marshall's. Thus, some confusion with locales is understandable; the town names are Masserberg, Schmiedefeld, Neuhaus am Rennweg, and Nordhalben (there is indeed a "Nordhausen," but it is many miles to the north, well beyond the regiment's area of operations).

Nordhausen [Nordhalben] was one of the shabbiest spots we had seen on our march across the country. The stench emanating from enormous muckheaps and ever-present outhouses was overwhelming. Scruffy women and grubby children drifted aimlessly up and down the streets, moving aside only when a jeep rolled by. That night, revolted by the filth around us, we unanimously refused to sleep in the so-called beds. Bob Jenkins was completely disgusted, and required a bottle of spirits to restore his own spirit. Of course, all the rest of us needed a little picking up, too …

About the only good thing I can recall from our stay in that village was the presence of a playable radio. Several swing fans—Joe Vella, Angelo Nicolo, Myles Fulmer, and I—sat up almost 'til morning listening to music and the news being broadcast by the BBC in London.

We departed that hellhole at first light. Everyone was anxious to get to our next stop for several reasons: one was the fact that our battalion was to be put in reserve there (*hallelujah!*); another was that the town where we were to be billeted, Dörnthal, was situated on one of Hitler's prized superhighways, the *autobahn*. About four o'clock in the afternoon our vehicles were rolling down this expressway, which proved to be an excellent piece of construction indeed; in many respects it resembled the famed Merritt Parkway in Connecticut and the Boston Turnpike. Our temporary home in Dörnthal was a large, castle-like building with plenty of room to set up the station and sleep.

We moved into town on April 13 for a pleasant, restful two days during which time Edward Conley rejoined us after having spent a week on R and R on the French Riviera.[2] His colorful tales of the high life made us wish we had been there with him. Instead, we had to settle for taking a great number of pictures of the nearby buildings and scenery where we were. It seems that while he was enjoying himself at the famous resort, Conley man-

---

2. Based on the author's chronology and the regiment's verifiable movements, the relocation to Dörnthal more likely occurred on April 14.

aged to lose all his clothes (except those on his back), money, and personal items—due, no doubt, to the gentle Mediterranean breezes—never because of the *jeunes filles* or the liquor found there in abundance. Quite a character, this young, copiously decorated lad.

Two days later we moved a few miles south into the reserve regimental assembly area in Lipperts and set up leisurely in a local house. No sooner had we arrived than we experienced an unfortunate accident. A curious German civilian lost both hands and an eye from an American grenade he had regarded as a plaything; a tragic affair to be sure, but he was lucky to be alive. These things happen in war. Although it was now clear that we were nearing the end of our long ordeal, the senseless brutality of it all left its scars on everyone.

Our stay there was a very pleasant one. The day after we arrived, we were surprised by the appearance of a mobile Red Cross unit bringing coffee, donuts, music—and best of all—American speech and girls. To top off a very delightful afternoon, we all squeezed into a gymnasium to see a movie, *Janie*,[3] enjoyable even though everyone had seen it many times before. Much to our dismay, the projectionist, Abie Interest, screwed up the film several times. Never had he shown a complete film without something happening, so everyone expected the worst (and usually got it!).

Of course, we continued to enjoy *beaucoup* eggs in Lipperts. These "snacks" in addition to the army chow kept us happy. In order to add to our egg ration, Ferdinand Bruegge paid social calls to all of the kitchens in the vicinity and returned with the

---

3. *Janie* might have been the only film available, but at least it was a recent release (September 1944). A romantic comedy featuring a high-spirited ingénue and the young soldiers at the local army base ("She's the gleam in the eye of every GI"), it was the perfect fare for a bunch of homesick American boys. In the promo materials, Warner Bros. boasted, "We've made a lot of pictures … that reflected America's greatness. But *Janie*, as much as *Destination Tokyo* or *The Adventures of Mark Twain*, is a rousing cheer for the things that make America *American* … and another example of how to combine "good picture-making with good citizenship."

ingredients for making spaghetti. This meant that our Italian friends, Joe Vella, Nicolo, and George Trabucco, went to work–their genuine Italian food had gained everyone's respect. To top off our supper that night, Captain Dedick produced several bottles of good American scotch, and they were duly consumed. We retired to our lodgings with full stomachs and peaceful thoughts.

Jumping off and out of reserve on April 18, we headed south toward our next division objective, the storied Danube River. Until this day, we had been following a generally southeastward course from Suhl toward the strong citadel of Hof. We medics were fortunate enough to have access to vehicles (we had two jeeps, a truck, and an ambulance), making the day's work pleasant—we cruised down the autobahn for about fifteen miles to Berneck.[4] Our drivers, including Joe Vella, Jenkins, and Waryasz, were really in their glory as they rolled down this excellent highway; it certainly was a change from the back roads on which we usually traveled. After negotiating much rough terrain, these men deserved a little easy driving.

Along the way, we received some incoming German shells. We had to hole up outside a town while our vaunted artillery silenced the interruption. This they accomplished in short order, and our advance party—the jeep and four men—rolled on into town to select a good, clean *gasthaus* for our aid station setting. After telling the jovial proprietor to get a move on, we plopped down to rest a moment while awaiting the arrival of the aid station proper. Our host happily complied, presenting two frothy steins of beer, which to his astonishment were firmly refused by Waryasz and me. To silence his insistent pleas, we coolly informed him that we thought the beer might be poisoned and that we would drink only after him. He did and we did.

One incident occurred that day that will not soon be forgotten—we were strafed for the second time in the war by two Ger-

---

4. Bad Berneck.

man Me 109s.[5] They swooped down suddenly on the rear of our column. We were scared stiff, but that didn't prevent us from getting the hell out of that vicinity. We scooted under some trees in a flash. Just behind our medical vehicles one of our supporting antiaircraft crews opened up on the Jerries, shooting one of them down. We gingerly made our way back to the jeep. Everyone was grinning rather self-consciously, talking boldly about how unconcerned they were about the matter. There was a shallow, swiftly running mountain stream flowing alongside the road, but not one medic got wet crossing the stream and running for cover. We had to laugh when we found out that Captains Streepey and Mumme (HQ Company CO) had dived right into the middle of the stream in their efforts to find cover. They were both soaked to the skin, much to our amusement.

Our idle chatter was cut short by a shout for medics. Throwing a couple of litters on the jeep, Warren Watkins, Jenkins, Vella, and I took off in the direction of the call. Our patient was a French slave worker in a nearby glass factory who had been slightly wounded by shell fragments from one of our tanks. Amid much praise and torrents of tears from his fellow workers, we loaded him on our jeep litter rack. We passed out cigarettes to some men of the 101st Engineers, then we drove back to the ambulance with our casualty to start him on his route of evacuation.

As we were loading another casualty (a young lady) into the ambulance, she shyly informed us that she needed to answer the call of nature, so Joe Vella quickly volunteered to help her in her time of need. Lifting her up tenderly from the litter, he carried her to a nearby outhouse, which they both entered. Several moments later they both exited, Vella looking a little bit sheepish about the whole affair.

---

5. The Messerschmitt Bf 109 (popularly known as the Me 109), workhorse of the Luftwaffe, appeared in a number of variations throughout its long service history. Variously armed with a battery of bombs, machine guns, and cannon, as well as the capability to fire rockets, the Bf 109 was certainly something to be feared. It was in a Bf 109G-14 that Luftwaffe ace Maj. Erich Harmann scored his unrivaled total of 352 confirmed kills.

We all managed to get a bath in a modern bathtub while we were in Berneck. The only European thing about it was the fact that the water had to be heated in a boiler alongside the tub, then pumped from the tank into the tub. After fixing everything up, Larry Hrouda found himself last in the line that formed from out of nowhere. When we left the next morning for a town called Plössen, at least we were clean.

This village proved to be only four or five modest farmhouses with connecting barn and pigpen and the commonly found high manure pile out front. Immediately after setting up, Menard, Jenkins, and I departed to check the position of the companies and to gather enough eggs for our next meal, as was our custom. We found the eggs easily enough, but we had to rely on helpful civilians for directions to the companies. While riding around the countryside, we stumbled upon the remains of a German airfield. Wrecked planes littered the runway; huge, 500-pound bombs were scattered across the field; and at one end stood the steel skeleton of a hangar. Numerous bomb craters attested to the fact that even this small airstrip had been given proper attention by our excellent air corps. It took about two hours to complete our tour of the neighborhood. With our reconnoitering concluded, we returned to the aid station.

Immediately after arriving at our new digs, I strolled out to the foul-smelling barn to chat up a cute little Polish milkmaid. But as I approached the door, it was evident that our own Polacks—Geisler and Waryasz—had the situation well in hand. I walked back into the station a bit crestfallen and hit the sack. Such a good kid!

Just before we left Plössen, Captain Dedick returned to duty to replace Captain Streepey. Before anyone could say hello or goodbye, Streepey had his gear in the ambulance and was leaving. A short while later, the advance party headed out, following the troops as usual, but this time they were in a happy mood because everyone was glad to see our regular boss back in the saddle.

As usual, our advance crew, tired of merely creeping along behind the slow-moving foot troops, dashed on ahead into the next town, Kemnath. The crew comprised Lieutenant Richardson and some enlisted men—Jenkins, Gomer Dancy, and me. We were well known throughout the battalion for our devil-may-care attitude; yet what was perceived as recklessness had saved many a wounded GI during the war.

Our first view of Kemnath was truly remarkable: it had been the recipient of a devastating working-over by both our air corps and artillery, and only a couple of buildings were left standing in the entire place. Every home was either still burning or in complete shambles. The people remaining in the city were walking slowly up and down the battered streets in a daze. Piles of debris littered the streets.

In one of the two houses that were still relatively intact, we were greeted at the door by an American GI. He claimed he had lost his outfit—a tank company—and was just waiting for friendly troops to show up. He looked suspiciously like an AWOL, especially since he was half-potted and had a comely farm girl at his elbow. Before we had a chance to scout around for a suitable station house, we were forced to beat a hasty retreat by a long burst of machine-gun fire that ricocheted from the ruins with terrible screeching noises. We really screwed out of that territory fast and were dumbfounded to find out later that the firing came from our own infantrymen preparatory to their entering the town. *Thanks, fellas!*

That night we stayed in a priest's home. This practice of occupying the church homes was frowned upon by our officers, but that night it was a case of necessity. We whiled away the hours by banging on the piano and small organ that we found in the house. Barney Menard, Herbie Scheinberg, and I nearly got pitched out on our ear on this account. The men were no music lovers, I guess.

Andy Dedick and John Waryasz. Photo courtesy of Ann Hall Marshall.

Staff Sergeants German and Bruegge, 1945. Photo courtesy of Ann Hall Marshall.

The following day, the captain and I took some photographs of the battered city to make a record of the destruction for posterity. We then pushed on southward to our next goal. The territory in this section of Germany was very scenic and beautiful, especially at sunrise and sunset. Now that the enemy had seemingly given up the battle in this sector, it was possible to again enjoy the peaceful things in life. However, every hill or gully was looked upon with a military eye—easy terrain to hold, poor evacuation routes, etc.

The next four or five days passed somewhat monotonously. Everyone was always tired when we stopped for a night's rest in such quaint watering holes as Zell and Hohenberg. By this time we were very close to the Danube, so naturally our spirits began to rise. As we entered Steinach they soared![6] The town was untouched by shells, and here again were many liberated Russian, French, and Polish forced laborers, all gleefully looting the houses right in front of their former German overseers. Pretty frauleins strolled the streets, and our scavengers (Martin, Cohen, and Fulmer) found the egg hunting to be excellent! After learning of the horrors that had been committed by the Nazis in this district, we again turned our eyes away while looters "looked over" the home in which we were billeted. They went about their task quite thoroughly; after they left, the place looked like a cyclone had hit it.

Albert Caproni, the regimental mail clerk, brought in an armload of mail, so everyone was ecstatic. Paul Yee, our Chinese aidman in Dog Company, returned from the hospital and left immediately for his company.

Much to our chagrin, we remained only six hours in Steinach; we were then ordered to move on by a division advance

6. About the time that German and his cohorts arrived in Steinach, elements of the 328th took Field Marshal Paul Ludwig Ewald von Kleist into custody in nearby Mitterfels. Because of his high rank, it was considered something of a coup for the unit. Von Kleist was a Prussian noble of the old school who had never gotten along well with the Führer; he had been sacked by Hitler in the spring of '44 and had been living quietly in retirement at his home in Mitterfels when the Allies arrived on the scene.

party. This alone signified to us that no enemy resistance was near, since this was the first time in over seven months that the "rear-echelon commandos" had caught up with us.[7]

All of the companies were put on trucks and we rolled out. Our first glimpse of the muddy, brown, slow-moving Danube River occurred on April 29 as we entered the riverside resort town of Bogen, another temporary halting point in the day's travel. While waiting for further orders, I accompanied Lieutenants Warrick and Williams on an exploration of a beautiful castle located high on a mountain overlooking the river.[8]

After a rough climb up the mountainside, we finally reached our goal. It was breathtaking to gaze upon the winding river with the stately Bavarian Alps as a backdrop. The mountaintops were capped with snow and the change of climate was noticed by all of the men. The riverbank was littered with the hulks of barges sunk by the Heinies.

We hated to leave such a poetic setting, but war is war. As we had ascended the mountain trail, there had been a few bursts fired from a stray burp gun on the opposite bank of the river, so naturally we descended using a different route. Charlie Company was saved from having heavy casualties when the Germans blew up a bridge only fifty yards in front of them. It was not our duty to cross the river at that point, so the company withdrew, secure in the fact that the Heinies would be dealt with by the 71st Division, which was cleaning out that section of the country.

When we returned to the jeep, there were three crates of eggs resting in the backseat—our boys were excellent scavengers. Again we rolled on, finally arriving in Niederwinkling to spend the night. It was just as well that we spent the entire night here,

---

7. The reader should not conclude that the fighting was over—far from it. As the regiment moved through each of these towns and villages, it met resistance of varying degrees of intensity. On April 26, the 2nd Battalion met stubborn resistance before it took Metten and the following day, it fought under an artillery barrage and sniper fire for four hours while it cleared Deggendorf.
8. Bogen is situated at the base of a hill called the Bogenberg. Atop his eminence rests a famous pilgrimage church, the *Wallfahrtskirche Sankt Maria Himmelfahrt*. As there is no castle in the environs, and since the church (the oldest pilgrimage church in Bavaria) is an imposing edifice in its own right, this may be the building the author is referring to.

because on the following day we pushed into the large town of Deggendorf, where we enjoyed one of the rare, excellent times of the war. Our "holiday" was only interrupted by some random shellfire from a German tank hidden along the bank across the river.

Just after we entered the city, Fulmer, Vella, and I decided to have some fun. We walked into one of the German Army hospitals and asked to be shown through the wards by the commanding officer. After we convinced him that we were U.S. inspecting officers, this wish was granted, and so, escorted by a major, three captains, and a gaggle of other ranks, we examined various patients, always asking pertinent questions about their injuries. We really enjoyed ourselves.

Later we moved into a nice home. The scavenger squad was turned loose, Jenkins and Waryasz in the lead. The cellar yielded the prize—three cases of Weinbrand[9] and champagne. That night everyone in the aid station joined in one of our now-famous parties, which was still going on at four o'clock the next morning. It was a standard policy at some time during our parties to put on a spontaneous stage show. These were usually built around Martin Cohen and Herbie Scheinberg. We had one of the best emcees I have ever seen or heard in Martin Cohen; when he starts speaking, everyone has to laugh. Going down the roster—we enjoyed Scheinberg's dancing, Italian songs by Vella, more warbling by Trabucco and "The Voice" (James Rullo, aka the Joisy Kid), track information by Geisler and Nicolo, piano hits by Menard, and so on into the night. These acts were always in rare form when everyone was half-polluted. Needless to say, the show that night was a smash hit. It was one of those real stag parties that will never be forgotten. It took three days for the fellows to recover from its effects.

By that time, we had passed through Hengersberg and found ourselves in a unique situation: the night's lodging and aid sta-

---

9. A type of German brandy.

tion consisted of one room plus an attic—that was no problem, but the catch was that in our one room was an elderly, invalid lady who could not move from her bed. So for the first time in this peculiar war, we slept "legally" in mixed company. However, we were gallant soldiers, so we slept with our clothes on. We were very happy to clear out the following afternoon. Before we left, Charlie Company brought in an entire regiment of Hungarian soldiers as PWs with all their equipment intact and their wives in tow. Good army tactics? *Ich weiss nicht!*[10]

On May 4 we achieved the crowning success of the war from the publicity angle—our regiment, the 328th Infantry, aided by the 11th Armored Division, captured Austria's third largest city, Linz.[11] The famous city capitulated after a conference between our commanding officer, Colonel Menard and the German commandant of the city's defenses. He approached our lines in true war-movie fashion, carrying a huge white flag of truce.

They met on the side of a hill, saluted, and then began to discuss terms. The companies were ordered to hold fast to their positions until the conference was over. At first the German officer didn't like the sound of "unconditional surrender," but he quickly changed his mind when the colonel threatened to order every piece of artillery in the regiment to open up on Linz. He wasn't bluffing either, and everyone knew it, including the enemy. Following the written terms of surrender, the machine-gun section of Dog Company rode back into the city with him to receive the formal surrender. We trusted these Germans only as far as we could throw them, and sometimes not even that far. Right

10. Literally "I don't know"—the German equivalent of a French shrug.

11. Linz bore the dubious distinction of being Adolf Hitler's hometown. He had conceived a grandiose plan to develop Linz into the Reich's cultural hub, including a massive *Führermuseum* to house the artwork he had been methodically pilfering all across Europe. It was at Linz that General Patton had his historic meeting with his Soviet counterpart on May 12.

German was being a bit cheeky to suggest that his infantry *regiment* was "aided" by an armored *division*. In point of fact, the 328th had been temporarily attached to the 11th Armored; it reverted to the control of the 26th Infantry Division on May 7.

behind the machine guns went our jeep carrying Lieutenant Richardson, Menard, Cohen, Vella, and me. We entered an untouched metropolis, complete with sidewalks, paved streets, apartment houses, banks, and thousands of silent people.[12] Our feelings cannot be described by mere words.

As the enemy troops, under guard, marched down to our troops, I managed to grab a Luger pistol from one of them, my first such souvenir of the war. Soon the army photographers arrived, clicking their shutters at the happy doughboys and tankers who were already looking around town. We drove through the white-flagged streets looking over everything in sight for the next hour. It was really a nice town, and almost made us believe we were in the good ol' U.S. of A. Our aid station was set up quickly in a beautiful, three-story apartment home decorated with gorgeous tapestries and high-end furniture. As soon as we were settled in, everyone went out for a leisurely stroll to look the place over. Within a few hours the food began to pour in to our new quarters: Conley and Albert Daigle brought meat, Ferdinand Bruegge furnished the bread, and so on, so a big feast was prepared by our regular aid station cooks, Frank Valiga and Harry Winner. These two men proved themselves to be very capable chefs throughout the war; in the difficult times, their coffee and chow fortified both patients and aidmen.

Linz proved to be our easternmost position in the war; in the face of the advancing Red Army, we turned north toward Czechoslovakia, the sixth country to be occupied by the Yankee Division. Every day brought countless rumors about the end of the war to our expectant ears. We could sense that it wouldn't be long now.

After a couple of wonderful days of rest and relaxation in Linz, we hit the road again. On May 8, 1945, we stopped for the

---

12. The city center remained intact, but the Allies had executed a devastating bombing mission on the city's benzol (oil) plant in October 1944, and another on the city's massive marshalling yards only days before (April 25) the capitulation.

night in a small village just outside the Czech border.[13] It was late afternoon on the following day, in this pastoral setting of peace and contentment, that we received the news: the once-mighty German Reich had formally surrendered! The Wehrmacht had finally been beaten to the ground by the combined land, air, and sea forces of the United States and its allies.

We had been engaged in a friendly poker game at the time, and after digesting the news, we simply resumed our play. There was no cheering, no toasts, just a calm realization that at long last the ghastly conflict was over. Everyone present was relieved to be alive.

Shortly after receiving this news, Chaplain Gordon, Chaplain Solliday (both Protestant), and Father Bransfield (Catholic), held a large church service that was attended by everyone in the vicinity. All wanted to thank God for their salvation and ask for His blessing.

---

13. This is likely the Austrian village of Wullowitz, which is right on the Czech border on the highway running north out of Linz and through Freistadt.

At Boemisch Roren, Czechoslovakia, 1945

Back row, left to right: Touchette, Cacchia, Rullo, Menard
Front row, left to right: Waryasz, Geisler, Daigle

Back row, left to right: Martin, German, Schienberg, Cacchia,
Rullo (top), Melnicoff (below)
Front row, left to right: Milky, Waryasz, Geisler, Trabucco

Photos courtesy of Ann Hall Marshall.

Epilogue

[THEA MARSHALL NOTES: As I was finalizing this book, I came across the following piece by my father. It seemed the perfect epilogue! The main body of the text underwent several rounds of professional editing (paragraphing/chaptering, stylistic consistency, grammar/syntax, etc.) to optimize readability. By contrast, I'm including (at the eleventh hour) this happy story very much as Dad wrote it, with minimal editing.]

Germany, May 1945

Andy & Kate, Freyung

Photos courtesy of Dedick family.

We spent time inside Czechoslovakia at
Boemisch Roren, where we had a wonderful event:
Kate Golden and Andy Dedick were married in the
village church by Father Bransfield, the 328th
chaplain!

Andrew Paul Dedick had gone straight from
his internship into the army and was assigned
to Lawson General Hospital in Georgia where he
met Kate Golden, an Army Nurse. After less than
two dozen days the romance was rudely
interrupted when Andy was sent to the 26th
Division to be a battalion surgeon in the 1st
Battalion of the 328th Regiment, good old
Handcar Red. Yours truly arrived at about the
same time--early summer of 1944--to be assistant
surgeon, heaven help us!

Andy and I got to be good friends and it
was a busy summer for all concerned. Kate
worked in a surgical team and went ashore over
the Utah Beaches a couple of days after the
initial landings on June 6. Handcar Red and our
sister components came over the same beaches
much later towards the first of September.

While we made our first all out attack
early in November, we were in static combat
positions all thru October. This would have been
in the vicinity of Nancy in Lorraine. When we
hauled casualties into the aid station, Andy and
our four technicians, Warren Watkins, Ferdinand
Bruegge, Dan Cacchia, and Angelo Nicolo, patched
them up so that they would be transportable to
the rear, where they would be treated by
skilled surgeons and their supporting staff of
nurses.

One night in October a returning ambulance
driver delivered a note for Lt. Dedick from
none other than Kate Golden, who was working in
the field hospital attached to the 26th. She
had seen his name on the tags attached to the
badly wounded that were coming her way. This
was indeed a battlefield romance! However,
neither party had the leisure to do much about
it until the following January when one of our
own AWOLs was caught and hauled before a court-
martial at division HQ. Since we were in a
holding position at the time, Andy and I were
summoned back to testify.

The ride back in the jeep was a cold one,
and we stopped by to see Kate. I was duly
introduced and dismissed to one side while Andy
and Kate picked up where they had left off back
in Lawson General.

The court was the next day, but we
proceeded back that evening to be on hand in
the A.M. The romance was in full bloom, so we
again stopped by Kate's hospital on our way
back.

That was all during hostilities, but
afterwards the faint sound of wedding chimes
began to fill our air. Kate's outfit was near
enough to us wherever we were, so the first
thing you know, while we were in Boemisch
Roren, Kate and Andy married!

Andy's father was a Greek Orthodox priest
back in Mt. Carmel, Penna.; this made Andy
Greek Orthodox, but he decided to jump the low
fence separating those worthy religionists from
Roman Catholics--he called on Tony DeVito and me
as sponsors. We in turn tossed a coin to see who

would be which, which is how I got to be Andy's
godfather, while Tony was his godmother! I was
also lucky to be chosen as best man. We have a
short videotape from a movie film of the event.

The regiment finally settled in Linz,
where we had fine accommodations. Andy and I
shared an apartment in the Herman Goering
Apartments on the first floor.

We each had a bedroom with a common bath
and kitchen. Tony DeVito spent a lot of time
with our battalion so he bunked with me. Kate
was able to get around regularly for a conjugal
visit with Andy. Indeed, one of their major
projects was getting Kate pregnant, so that she
would not be eligible for trans-shipment to
Japan where surgical skills were certain to be
in demand. We all worried a good deal about
going to Japan as a unit until the August
surrender of those worthy warriors.

I was antsy about getting back to the USA
and our family of three.

I had sailed to Europe on the Santa Maria
and finally, docked in Boston Harbor on Columbus
Day--Oct 12, 1945. Shades of history!

                                --Robert T. Marshall

Rosters

AS ROBERT MARSHALL NOTED: *"The medical detachment of the 1st Battalion, 328th Infantry Regiment, 26th Infantry Division [the Yankee Division] was a tiny cog in the Third Army ... led by Gen. George S. Patton, 'Old Blood and Guts.'"*

This small company of medics—about 45 men—braved the battlefields of Europe during WWII, from the Normandy Beaches to the Battle of the Bulge and beyond.

Conquering mud and blood, saving lives while struggling to stay sane, these courageous young men endured some of the fiercest fighting of the WWII, until the peace was won.

They impacted countless people—Americans, Frenchmen, Belgians, and more—in Europe.

Those that survived and made it home also helped create strong communities, touching many lives. For example:

- Bob Marshall became a professor in Maryland and taught over 5,000 students
- Walt German delivered 9,000+ Missouri babies
- Andy and Kate Dedick treated thousands of patients over the years in their New Jersey clinic

These healers and heroes had parents, spouses, friends, and everyone else they were connected to. Originally from Connecticut, Illinois, Massachusetts, Maryland, Missouri, New Jersey, New York, Ohio, Pennsylvania, Rhode Island, Tennessee, Wisconsin, and Washington, D.C., these valiant young soldiers eventually had connections in all fifty states, and other countries.

Check the following rosters or **healersandheroes.com** to find *your* connection to these courageous medics.

Roster of Men in the 1st Bn Aid Station: Initial Position in Normandy

1.	1st Lt Andrew P. Dedick	Mt. Carmel, PA
2.	2nd Lt Robert T. Marshall	Johnstown, PA
3.	Staff Sgt Daniel Cocomazzi	Boston, MA
4.	William Walls	Uniontown, PA
5.	T/3 Warren Watkins	Delaware, OH
6.	T/3 Ferdinand Bruegge	Breese, IL
7.	T/3 Daniel Chacchia	Geneva, NY
8.	T/5 Angelo Nicolo	North Providence, RI
9.	Pfc John Waryasz (driver)	Greenfield, MA
10.	Pfc Paul Compagnone (driver)	Lawrence, MA
11.	Pfc Robert Jenkins (driver)	Waymart, TN
12.	Pfc Frank Valiga	Linden, NJ
13.	Pfc Henry Menard (clerk)	Salem, MA
14.	Pfc Charles Touchette	Marlborough, MA
15.	Pfc George Trabucco	Providence, RI
16.	Pfc Dennis Madden	Jamaica Plains, MA
17.	Pfc Lawrence Honaker	Harrisburg, PA
18.	Pfc Joseph Vella	New Haven, CT
19.	Pfc Sam Solomon	New York, NY
20.	Pfc Herbert Schienberg	New York, NY
21.	Pfc James Kallal	Chicago, IL
22.	Pfc Edward Geisler	Westfield, MA

Roster of Men in the 1st Bn Aid Station:
Final Position in Oberhaid, Czechoslovakia

1.	Capt Andrew P. Dedick	Mt. Carmel, PA
2.	1st Lt Robert T. Marshall	Catholic University, Washington, D.C.
3.	Staff Sgt Walter German	U.S. Veterans' Hospital Jefferson Barracks, MO
4.	Cpl Robert Jenkins	Waymart, TN
5.	T/3 Warren Watkins	Columbus, OH
6.	T/3 Ferdinand E. Bruegge	Breese, IL
7.	T/3 Daniel Cacchia	Geneva, NY
8.	T/4 Angelo Nicolo	North Providence, RI
9.	T/5 John Warzasz	Greenfield, MA
10.	T/4 Martin Cohen	Lorain, OH
11.	T/5 Albert J. Daigle	Lawrence, MA
12.	T/5 James Rullo	Newark, NJ
13.	T/5 Myles Fulmer	Westfield, WI
14.	T/5 Joseph E. Vella	New Haven, CT
15.	Pfc Samuel Melnicoff	Syracuse, NY
16.	Pfc Herbert Scheinberg	New York, NY
17.	Pfc Edward Conley	Waterview, MD
18.	Pfc Edward Geisler	Westfield, MA
19.	Pfc George Trabucco	Providence, RI
20.	Pfc Frank Valiga	Linden, NJ
21.	Pfc Charles Touchette	Marlborough, MA
22.	Pfc Henry E. Menard	Salem, MA
23.	Pfc Henry W. Winner	Vandville, NJ
24.	Pfc Harold Martin	Oregon, IL
25.	Pfc Gomer Dancy	no address

Biographical Information

Capt. Robert T. Marshall

Born: Johnstown, PA

Education:
Tioga St. Grammar School, Johnstown, PA
Johnstown Catholic High School, Johnstown, PA
BA: St. Vincent College, Latrobe, PA
MA/PhD: Catholic University, Washington, DC

Instructor: Industrial Arts
St. Joseph High School, Emmitsburg, MD

Professor:
Classical Languages, Ancient History, Linguistics
Mt. St. Mary's College (now University), Emmitsburg, MD

Sgt. Walter A. German

Born: Kansas City, MO

Education:
BA/MD: Washington University, St. Louis, MO
Internship: Jackson Memorial Hospital, Miami, FL
Residency: Grady Memorial Hospital, Atlanta, GA

Practice:
Smith Glynn Callaway Clinic, Springfield, MO
Springfield hospitals, Springfield, MO

Capt. Andrew P. Dedick, Jr.

Born: Osceola Mills, PA

Education:
BA/MD: George Washington University, Washington, DC
Residency: Columbia Presbyterian Hospital, New York, NY
Director of Radiology, Riverview Medical Center, Red Bank, NJ

Practice: Red Bank, NJ

Retired: North Palm Beach, FL

Lt. Kathleen Golden Dedick

Born: Jersey City, NJ

Education:
RN: Jersey City Medical Center School of Nursing, Jersey City, NJ
Army Nurse Corps, 4th Auxiliary Surgical Group

Retired: North Palm Beach, FL

Dedick ~ Yankee Division, 26th Infantry, 328th Regiment, 1st Battalion

Golden ~ Army Nurse Corps, 4th Auxiliary Surgical Group, 16th Field Hospital

44' Dec.
Perle, Luxembourg

Afterword

AS NOTED in my Introduction, transforming my father's narrative into a book was challenging. Over the four years of this project, daunting obstacles caused me on a number of occasions to consider abandoning it. The three stories below illustrate a few of the hurdles encountered.

First Example

While discussing my work on Dad's book with Willie Jones, the 1997 World Champion Toastmaster and a member of my local club, he cautioned, "Be sure and get the military stuff right."

I blithely agreed to so do.

Later that day, I wondered what he'd meant. A talented local editor had converted the scanned copy into a decent Word document. What more was needed, other than breaking it into chapters, plus a few footnotes?

I *had* noted inconsistencies (Captain sometimes, Capt. others, and such), in Dad's oeuvre. Various reference manuals were both confusing and conflicting. After consulting a history buff friend, I'd decided to simply bypass the need to further research all that "stuff" and spell every title out in full—now I was concerned about that choice.

Willie was an Air Force veteran, so I buttonholed him at our next meeting, seeking clarification. He explained that military ranks, abbreviations, language, etc. are rigid and specific. Also, they differ among the branches *and* change over time. If I wanted the military audience (yes!), then "the military stuff" needed to be right. I thanked Willie, still clueless about what lay ahead.

Revisiting the style manuals led me to conclude that I needed yet *another* editor, one with extensive military and historical expertise.

I began the search for a willing, available, affordable military editor.

My network of colleagues and friends offered starting points. One source led to another. From Hawaii to Virginia, Seattle to NYC, and back to Hawaii; then, forward to London, Washington, D.C., and back to Virginia—I chased every lead.

Finally, five months later, when I was certain I couldn't bear to make one more call, send one more email, or handle one more rejection, there it was—a light at tunnel's end!

New contacts led me to Aden Nichols, a former Green Beret turned editor. He was more than I'd dared to hope for—he'd even organized a 50th anniversary parachute jump into Europe for a group of WWII vets.

Second Example

Graphics for the book involved on-going complications. Sometimes, events were so absurd that I had to laugh out loud.

From Mom I had small, black-and-white photos that Dad had sent from Europe. He'd labeled almost all of them on the back with valuable information—dates, names, and places.

The families of Walt German and Andy Dedick added to the treasure trove.

Great, I had my pictures.

Not so fast, a friend opined—get permissions from the two other families. *Written* permissions. I did so, though it took quite a bit of back and forth.

After reviewing the "final" graphics package, Aden suggested a few further additions—e.g., a poster for the movie *Janie*, referenced several times in the manuscript, and a stock photo of a Tommy gun, also addressed in detail.

I groaned, appreciative but overwhelmed—I'd happily relegated graphics to the "completed" pile.

Nevertheless, I accepted this advice and sought guidance on how best to proceed. Aden provided Warner Brothers' contact information for the *Janie* poster. *That* request fell flat—too expensive, too much paperwork.

He recommended the Fort Meade Military Museum for a stock Tommy gun photo at little or no cost, noting that director Robert Johnson had proven most helpful to him a few years earlier.

What follows is a snippet (11/02/17) from the voluminous correspondence with Aden about sourcing yet more graphics:

"... I mentally pep-talked myself on Tuesday at about 6:15 AM to call Ft Meade Museum—spoke with the "last woman standing"—they were closing <u>permanently</u> that day, director departed an hour earlier, files shipped or stored at various locales, curator of collections dead of a sudden heart attack two weeks earlier!

Last Woman Standing Barbara suggested contacting the 25th Infantry Division or gunbroker.com but I can't start down more rabbit holes.

Felt like it was a sign—punting on the Tommy gun unless you've some other idea. I see lots on "Pinterest royalty-free WWII tommy gun" but no idea what to do next. Attaching one screen shot for reference."

With Aloha, Thea

Luckily, such frustrations were often balanced by the efforts of my amazing "team"—e.g., Aden located a royalty-free stock photo of a Tommy gun.

Third Example

While pulling together the various components for the book, Mom and I frequently discussed strategies for its development and promotion. I did the bulk of the legwork, as I had with her novels, but I relied on Mom for clarification, expansion, decisions, information, and more. Further, her keen marketing instincts, honed over many years, would be a huge asset.

I sent Mom a selection of magazines that might review the book, or find its development worthy of coverage. The May 11, 2016 draft of a query letter she promptly composed and sent to me for consideration showcases Mom's savvy:

> *"During WWII, while all around them men were killing and being killed, soldiers in the front-line aid station risked their lives to rescue GIs lying wounded and helpless on the smoking battlefield.*

When WWII began, Robert Thomas Marshall (1919–1996) was drafted as a buck private during his first semester of graduate school. Four years later, he was discharged as a captain, with a Silver Star, Purple Heart, and four battle ribbons including the Battle of the Bulge. He was a medic in General Patton's third army. On his own initiative, my husband kept a log of what went on in the aid station. Surprisingly, that included an overseas romance. Dr. Andy Dedick, commanding officer of the aid station, married a nurse from the field hospital. Bob was best man.

I have the large, annotated maps on which my husband marked their route. I am 95 years old. My daughter Thea Marshall and I will soon publish a book titled *Healers and Heroes.* I will send you a copy. If this is of interest to your (magazine, program, newsletter) please contact me for further information.

Sincerely,
Ann Hall Marshall"

Mom proved a productive, effective partner, even from 6,000 miles away—I was now living in Hawaii and she was in Maryland. Mom was more pragmatist than perfectionist, but her standards were high. This book had to be well produced to truly honor my Dad.

On August 14, 2016, my Mom died at age 95. I'd known she was ill, and I'd been pushing hard to get the book published, certain that she would rally once again—she was excited to share my Dad's account with the world.

Her passing was a huge blow. Aside from the indescribable personal devastation, I lost my amazing book collaborator. Mom was my best resource—a fabulous writer and editor, as well as a constant source of inspiration and ideas about how to best proceed. In addition to her impressive problem-solving abilities, she'd also offered to underwrite much of the cost of bringing Dad's story to publication. How would I continue without all that support? Was it worth soldiering on? Should I? Could I?

No money, no military editor (yet), no viable website, no Mom for details and support.

Despite my despair, I ultimately decided to do what my Mom and Dad had always modeled for their ten children: Carry on. My folks wanted Dad's story out in the world.

My Dad wrote in his Preface:

This account of our day-by-day movements is naturally microcosmic, covering the actions of only a handful of men (and those with whom we came in immediate contact), but it is a tale that deserves to be told as much as many I've read covering the momentous events of those perilous years.

Problems be damned—I'd find that military editor (just one month later), punch through the numerous other roadblocks, and publish the book.

I felt overwhelmed, but determined. Not intrepid, but inveterate. I not only had to do the job well, but all the decisions from here on in would be mine alone. But I would prevail, even though the challenge was now greatly magnified.

More of my 4-year saga will be posted at the website **healersandheroes.com**, and in other publications.

It was a privilege to produce this work! Many positives emerged, despite the numerous impediments.

Internet searches led me to kindred spirits—WWII vets and their descendants.

An amazing young man in Florida, Ben Mack-Jackson, started a non-profit (WWII Veterans History Project) to preserve veterans' stories and educate the next generation.

The Battle of the Bulge Association is another organization dedicated to sharing and preserving the stories of the remarkable soldiers who fought in that pivotal battle.

Later this year, I hope to attend the 26th Yankee Division Reunion in New England. I can't wait to meet the children and grandchildren of my Dad's comrades.

My father wrote of carrying a fellow medic, Alfred Wilson, through the mud for an hour to the Aid Station—sadly, Alfred died of his grievous wounds, but was posthumously awarded the Medal of Honor. His niece, Carolyn McKinney, wrote a book, *The Gentle Giant of the 26th Division*. I met Carolyn by phone and was delighted to discover this unexpected connection. Her account of meeting and visiting with my parents at a Division reunion brought both tears and joy.

The "healers and heroes" I was honored to work with on this project seemed to reflect (in an easier setting) the spirit and values that drove the Allied forces to victory in WWII.

My Dad died at home, surrounded by family, in July, 1996. I still miss him deeply and wish he and my Mom were alive. I think of them every day. I find comfort because I know, with absolute certainty, that this book would please them.

—Thea Marshall
April, 2019

Acknowledgements

BRINGING THIS 1945 military manuscript into the 21st century for publication required an army of supportive people and I am tremendously thankful to them.

I'm grateful that my mother, Ann Hall Marshall, asked me to publish my father's story, an honor (and task) gladly accepted. Mom was a marvelous partner and an incredible font of wisdom, inspiration, and knowledge. Working on this book has been a privilege.

Lori Phillips and Diane Barbeler were incomparable guides when I lost the path after my mother's 2016 death. Missing materials? Lori's got my back! Organizing and curating? Diane to the rescue! And much more than can be detailed here.

Aden Nichols (Little Fire Publishing) was my fabulous military editor. Aden is a Renaissance man, with wide-ranging knowledge and expertise. His superb attention to detail was critical in making this book stylistically consistent and militarily sound. Special thanks to John D. Manley and Martha A. Hayes (The Dedicated Editor) for that connection.

Marcella and Andi (Spectrum Publishing) demonstrated creativity and flexibility in developing the cover design and graphics.

Dorri Olds (dorriolds.com) rode to the rescue! She stepped up with terrific aesthetics, skills, and professionalism, under tight timelines and difficult circumstances. She brought this book home. She is fabulous!

My writing group, the Waikiki Word Wranglers—Bob, Laureen, Gail, Joanna, Vicki, Marcia—were always spot-on and kind, offering constructive critiques. Bob Newell (an accomplished, published writer) armed me with needed tools to push ahead. Gail Baugniet, another talented author (check out her books on Amazon), is also especially gifted at copy-edits—she generously undertook an early detailed copyedit. (Back when I mistakenly thought the manuscript was ready to go.)

Kay Haring, an original Wrangler, now lives in Pennsylvania. As we forged ahead, she took the lead. Her book has been a best seller for over two years, consistently among Amazon's top 25 in Children's Art History. Kay has shared valuable lessons and hard-won insights.

Sincere appreciation goes to early readers/advisors Bob Snyder, Mickey Addison, John Greenwood, Richard Ginn, Rosemary Wolfe, Patrick Hinchy, and Steve Bury. Initial editing kudos to Erin Akiko Shishido, Professor Russell Hart, and my sister-in-law, Lois Paciello.

Tracey Meehan, Charley German, Anne Cannell, and the Dedick family gave welcome encouragement (and permissions) for this book. Many thanks to these individuals and families.

My dear friend Charlotte, who knows my family well, contributed much-needed perspective, support, and sagacity to keep me on track. I am truly grateful to her.

The Ala Moana Toastmasters group's ongoing enthusiasm for my Dad's story confirmed its relevance. Solid advice from Willie Jones, World Champion Toastmaster, motivated my search for a military editor (Aden Nichols, above).

Dr. Christopher Snedden's cogent counsel, often in collaboration with that of the above-mentioned Diane Barbeler, was invaluable. Glyphs, maps, cover, general organization—nothing was too small or large for their smarts and talents. That unstinting, multi-faceted help was an astonishing gift.

My siblings inspired me to aim higher, go deeper, and break through any barriers that I encountered—our Dad chronicled an important segment of American history, and I hope I have done it justice.

Mahalo to Seann for spotting the errant ampersands throughout. Also to Indi, Trish, Tami, Giny, Maryanne, and my entire posse—you guys rock. I truly appreciate the encouragement offered by so many individuals, not all of whom I can name here.

My husband, Ethan Allen, read and edited numerous revisions of the entire text, and provided a sounding board for my ideas and frustrations. His reliability and steadiness gave me the strength to soldier on. Ethan's simply the best.

I attended several events sponsored by the Luxembourg and Belgium embassies for WWII vets and families. Ambassadors Sylvie Lucas and Dirk Wouters (as well as Stan Myck and others) shared their countries' admiration for, and remembrances of, our WWII men and women. They have not forgotten, and still honor, the courageous service of our American veterans. Inspiration in spades!

While many made important suggestions and corrections, any errors that remain are my responsibility.

About the Editor

Thea Marshall

Born: Gettysburg, PA

Education:
St. Joseph's High School, Emmitsburg, MD
St. Joseph College, Emmitsburg, MD
New College, Sarasota, FL
Mt. St. Mary's College (now University), Emmitsburg, MD
University of Washington, Seattle WA

Entrepreneur: Speaker, Writer, Artist, Educator

Thea has created award-winning educational programs, exhibits, and products for many organizations, including the Smithsonian, FAO Schwarz,

Neiman Marcus, Harvard, National Science Foundation, SONY, Chicago's Museum of Science and Industry, et al.

Currently Vice-President of the Speakers Association of Hawaii and a certified Advanced Toastmaster, Thea has served on boards in Chicago, Seattle, and Honolulu.

In 2018, she was appointed to lead Public Relations for the international Battle of the Bulge Association that honors and preserves the legacies of veterans from that epic WWII battle.

Thea now lives in Hawaii with her scientist/educator husband, Ethan Allen.

Made in the USA
Middletown, DE
29 June 2019